Abandoned Justice:

The Cold Case of Ten-year-old Virginia Brooks

Book Three of the Colder Case Series

By
George Sherwood

Contents

Chapter 1: Walk to School 3

Chapter 2: Unspeakable 6

Chapter 3: The Search 16

Chapter 4: Tragic Find 36

Chapter 5: Forensic Science 65

Chapter 5: Conclusion? 93

Chapter 6: Reopenings 99

Apendix: *People v. Stone, 6 Cal.2d 62* 116

Visit the Author's Amazon Series Page 118

Chapter 1: Walk to School

A walk to school was nothing new for Virginia Brooks. She had done so many times since moving to San Diego, East San Diego actually. It was about 1.3 miles to Euclid school from where she lived at 5602 University Boulevard, which back then was out in the boondocks without any housing tracts to civilize the countryside. University Boulevard, the street she lived on and had to walk over, was not a busy boulevard then. There were few intersections and the road curved and snaked for the first half mile or so before straightening out.

There were rolling hills and Virginia's brother, who left her behind while riding his bicycle that morning of Feb. 11, 1931, crested a hill ahead of her. From there he looked back and saw her still walking. It is tempting to wonder if he teased her about how much faster and easier it would be for him to get to school. Brothers can do that sometimes. Or maybe he offered one last time to let her ride on the handle bars. Perhaps she declined because he had books and she had books and a lunch basket and she carried a bouquet for her teacher. A 10-year-old considerate enough to prepare a bouquet for her teacher wouldn't want to risk harming the delicate blooms.

John Brooks, Virginia's father had left for work in his truck that morning at about 7:15 a.m. to pick up a load at the municipal pier and hauled lath from a "coastwise steamer" on the docks. Virginia's mother kissed her goodbye at about 10 to 8 or soon thereafter. A man driving to work said he saw who he thought was Virginia as her brother rode his bicycle. A news article reported:

"The last person known to have seen the child the morning she disappeared was Walter E. Bell, house detective at the Pickwick hotel….. Bell, who lives in El Cajon, said he first passed the Brooks boy and then the little girl."

A detail like this provided a fork in the investigation and complicated the search because it was possibly very important.

As she evidently often did, up ahead, Virginia's friend Katie Lucero waited on a corner past the snakes and hills that were the road. The two schoolgirls may have become friends when they each played a role in a dramatization "concerning Siegfried and Brunhilda" – the story of warrior princess and Valkyrie who was cruelly deceived by her lover, Siegfried -- at Euclid elementary school earlier in the school year, when the fifth grade students participated in National Education Week in November of 1930. Virginia, being new to the area after moving from Portland, Or., would undoubtedly relish the blooming friendship. San Diego was growing in the 1930s, just as it had years previously, and many residents were new. Katie waited 10 minutes longer than usual before she gave up, thinking Virginia was not going to school that day. Maybe she was sick.

A man who worked a junk shop "several blocks" away from her house said he saw a schoolgirl resembling Virginia walking. Mrs. B.H. Ward, who lived on Radio Road before it was 54th Street, reported to authorities that she saw an old Ford coupe at the curbing on University Avenue just west of Radio Road. That would be about halfway to school and Virginia would have to pass him as she walked. Mrs. Ward didn't think anything of it until Virginia was reported missing and she realized Virginia's route would take her by the man sitting on the running board. She did not see Virginia get in the car. Mrs. Ward would often be called upon to check if suspects were the man she saw, especially if they had an old Ford coupe. If there was no eye witness identification, that could rule the suspect out of that scenario. That of course does not explain the sightings by the woman who thought she saw Virginia walking with a man.

It was C.L. Chandler that operated a "junk shop" several blocks from Virginia's home and he said he saw her walking. Radio Road was before Chandler's wrecking yard on the route, so if he saw her she was still walking and she did not get a ride from the man sitting on the running board. Elsewhere, as mentioned, another woman said she saw Virginia walking with a man. She seemed most certain of having seen Virginia and was able to provide a good description of the girl and the man. The girl she described was carrying bundles and she also described the clothes very well. None of these sightings at the time seemed nefarious enough to cause alarm or to report anything to the police. One first assumption was that Virginia went off the road to pick flowers because Fleurette Vigneault, a friend of Virginia's, said Virginia told her she planned to stop and pick some wild flowers for a school nature class.

Chapter 2: Unspeakable

In 1924 two young sisters were murdered and left in the Angeles Mesa of Los Angeles. That is covered in *Uncivil Twilight*. In 1937 two young sisters and their friend went missing and their brutalized bodies were found two days later. That is the subject of *Colder Case*. It is probable, as I argued there, that the wrong man was executed for that crime. In both of those cases evidence revealed in the official commutation investigations after trial pointed to wrongful convictions.

Unfortunately, the tragic find in this 1931 case is

all-too-similar.

Virginia Brooks was a white, elementary age girl.
She was strangled with the strapping of her own garment.
Her body was found in a lonely mesa.

There is something more haunting in an unsolved case of a murdered little girl than there is even when an equally horrible crime results in a wrongful execution. "At least they tried," it can be said about a wrongful conviction or execution. The San Diego police and authorities throughout California and the Western states did try, and tried their very best. The San Diego police and Sheriff's office united their efforts to find little Virginia Brooks when she went missing and vanished without a trace. When her body was found, the investigation was magnified in terms of forensic science that was cutting edge then but is routine today.

The Los Angeles Police Department loaned two of their top "criminologists" to help analyze the evidence. One was a "chemist" who sought trace evidence and another was a tire identification expert. A chemist then is what we might call a crime scene investigator now, one who analyzes trace evidence looking for clues.

The state of California Department of Justice also sent down two expert investigators from the Bureau of Identification and Investigation (BII). They were armed with the files of "known degenerates" who lived in the area. They would spend weeks on the case and then would have to divide their focus on new shocking cases in the area that were possibly related. Another murder occurred not too far north of where Virginia's Brooks' body was found. Louise Teuber, 17-years-old, was found hanging nearly nude at Black Mountain. Camp Kearney Mesa, where Virginia's body was dumped, was about half way to Black Mountain along the same route.

There were in fact a series of murders in San Diego within the span of a few months and newspapers would report the "spree" started with the murder of little Virginia Brooks. Newspapers would also report that the Virginia Brooks murder was reminiscent of the murder of Marian Parker in 1927. One alleged similarity, though false, was that both were morbidly mutilated. The crime scene photos in the William Edward Hickman trial were so disturbing members of the jury were "sickened by pictures of the dismembered body of Marian Parker" and they "burst into tears." Due to that crime a few years earlier, the Virginia Brooks investigation took on an urgency that equaled no other search for a child in San Diego's history.

It is amazing how similar the crime investigation techniques were in 1931 compared to today and the investigators even used the forensic tools of etymology and horticulture. There was also understanding of what is today called "criminal profiling." The terms were different, but the understanding of serial killers was there. It was understood that if the person who killed Virginia Brooks was like Hickman, convicted of murdering 12-year-old Marian Parker, the killer would kill again. It is hoped the San Diego Police Department will consider submitting the Virginia Brooks' caset to [The Vidocq Society](#).

That there was a "crank" leaving threatening notes only added to the San Diego terror. Understandably, mothers all over the county were protecting their children the best they could by not allowing them to walk alone. There was also an understanding of "stranger danger" and Virginia was often warned against getting into a car with a stranger without her 12-year-old brother with her. This was assuming that whoever picked up Virginia on her way to school, if anyone did, was a stranger. If there was any fault to the investigation it was in the tunnel vision assumption that a stranger picked her up. But the investigation, as it would today, regrouped and discarded all assumptions, starting over with fresh eyes after reinforcement from the state and Los Angeles arrived. Lieut. George Sears took over from Chief Hill, and he jettisoned all assumptions to concentrate on the facts. Still, the focus was on anyone who left town just after Virginia disappeared and any known degenerates, but every clew was checked and rechecked. (The word was spelled "clew" by the Los Angeles Times in the 30s. One of the notes to police noted below spelled it that way also. Did the writer live in L.A.?)

Every credible lead was followed and there were sightings of Virginia all over California and in many states. This is possibly a reflection of the unreliability of eyewitness identification, a number one cause of wrongful convictions. It is easy to see how someone could see a little girl somewhere and then see a picture of Virginia in the paper days later and make a connection. Despite the best intentions, the procedure was flawed enough to lead to false leads that had to be followed no matter how unlikely. An "Amber Alert" app with facial and license plate recognition abilities would likely be more reliable but it still wouldn't be full proof. It could be reliable enough to eliminate clear misidentifications so the police looking for a missing child could concentrate their efforts on more certain clues. In the Virginia Brooks case, the police followed leads all over the state and it wasn't until her body was found closer to her home of San Diego that the investigation gave that angle the priority it deserved. Of course, hindsight is 20/20 and no theory or clue was completely ignored.

This book, like my two previous books, depicts the unspeakable. We hold crimes like these against children in the utmost contempt not only because of the sickness of the crime, but also because an adult against a child can never be a fair fight, and so in addition to the revulsion of an assault on a child there is the terrorism, and the murderers of children commit terrorist acts. Indeed, terrorism could be a motive at times. In all three of these cases, the communities were terrorized.

The guilty person in the Virginia Brooks murder was obviously not born in 1931 and would probably have to be almost 100-years-old now. In other words, this book is not a murder mystery that will solve a cold case crime all the way to a conviction.

Rather, it is a colder case and the intent is to reveal the complications and challenges of searching for a missing child. For those who have not read the previous books in [The Colder Case Series](), a colder case is one in which the murderer of a child got away with murder, for whatever reason. Given what we know today about evidence and investigation, it is possible to make some good guesses of who was overlooked in the Brooks case. The police could have talked to their person(s) of interest on more than one occasion without even suspecting it. Who would be your guess? Perhaps the Virginia Brooks case, if reopened and solved, would lead to more efficient search and investigation techniques that will save children's lives. Everyone prefers happy endings when it comes to missing children cases.

Search is still on for 10-year-old Virginia Brooks of San Diego, Cal., who has been missing several weeks. An international as well as interstate search has been conducted for her.

Figure 2 Virginia's picture in the Los Angeles Evening Herald. None of the pictures ever depicted a broken tooth.

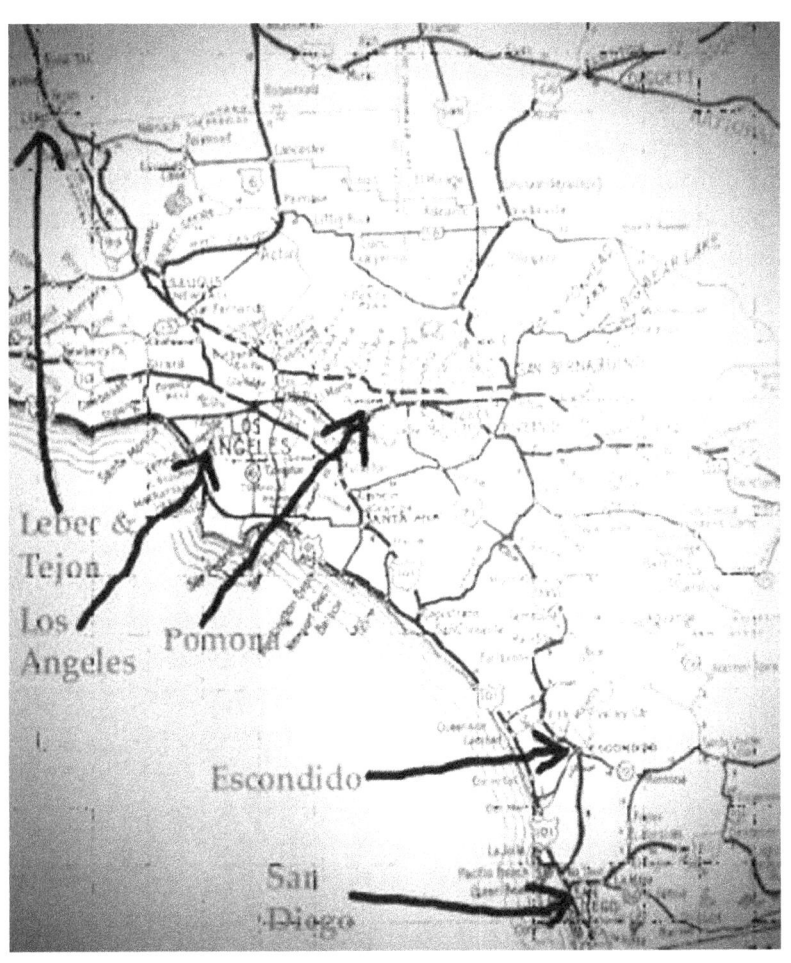

Figure 1 Southern California from San Diego to Lebec.

Figure 3 (opposite page): Map of Virginia's neighborhood. It was more barren of development in 1931. Walking from her home, Virginia normally would first pass Radio Rd./54th Street, then the junkyard, then meet Katie Lucero at Winona Ave, then go to school on Euclid Ave.

Abandoned Justice

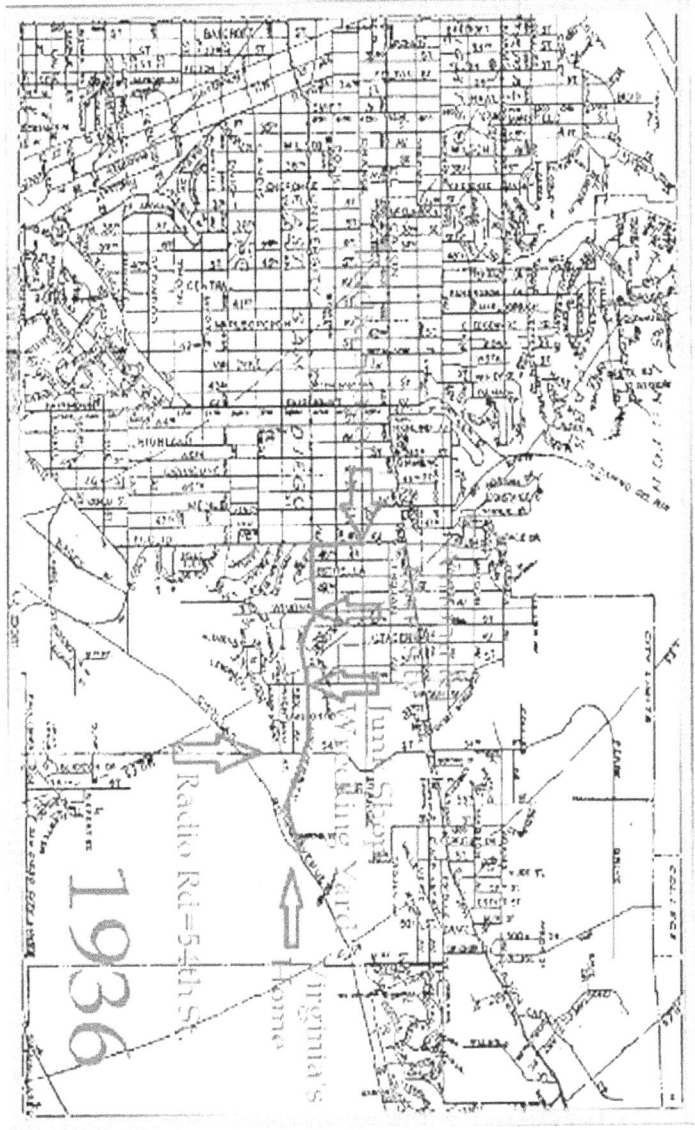

Chapter 3: The Search

Katie Lucero was supposed to meet Virginia at the corner of Winona Avenue and University; about 0.8 miles from Virginia's home, and Virginia did not make it. About half block east of Winona there is a bend in the road that obscures the line of sight, so the wrecking yard "junk shop" that was about half a mile east of there was not visible from where Katie stood. At first the police assumed Virginia disappeared within that distance of her home because she never met Katie. In addition to combing the mountains and ravines and brush of the surrounding area, the authorities had to ask if she may have been picked up by someone.

The talk and reporting of other crimes could not have been encouraging. Virginia's family was probably already kicking themselves for not doing something differently. If only. *If only I'd given her a ride.* Her father and her brother probably felt that guilt and it would likely fester. In addition to the fear and hope, there would be the guilt.

The Brooks had just moved to San Diego from Portland, Ore., about six months prior, no doubt looking for a better life. Like the Martin sisters of the 1924 murders and the Everett sisters of the 1937 murders, Virginia's parents undoubtedly thought they were moving someplace safe. Mr. And Mrs.

Everett must have thought the location in Inglewood perfect, half a block from a big park that was well supervised and a few blocks from school. So the 1931 news reports recounting the story of Nicholas Esparza, the 11-year-old boy whose body was found in Camp Kearny Mesa a few years before, and the reported similarities of the Marian Parker case, had to weigh on the Brooks family. As one paper reported, "Officers pointed out the girls were nearly the same age and Hickman followed the Parker girl to school, said her father had sent him, and persuaded her to leave."

Police Sergeant E.C. Griffith was initially in charge of the search. He focused on a lost child search and organized search parties accordingly. While he couldn't discount the possibility she was kidnaped like the other children mentioned in the newspapers, he was fairly certain it was not a kidnap for ransom case as the Brooks family was struggling, like many during the depression, and did not have a lot of money.

It wasn't long before there were sightings.

On the 13th of February, the 3rd day of Virginia being missing, her aunt Lilly Campbell went down to San Diego from Los Angeles. The Brooks did not have a picture of Virginia and Mrs. Campbell took one down. It wasn't long before there was a picture to add to the physical description in the newspapers, but even the picture was vague. She looked like a 10-year-old girl with a bob haircut, which was likely the most popular then. There is some bitter irony in the fact that Mrs. Martin bobbed May's hair the day she disappeared in 1924. It was fashionable in 1924 and May Martin was supposed to meet her aunt who was going to marcel her newly bobbed hair. A wavy bob was most popular.

A man who lived next door to a store, A. Homes of 1226 India Street, reported he saw a girl in a car with a couple. The man parked in front of the store next door to Homes' house and jumped out to quickly get a paper. The couple scanned the front page and then drove off. The girl with them closely resembled Virginia and she was crying and upset. Mr. Homes thought the girl was being held against her will.

As we will see, there would be many sightings like that and every one had to be followed to conclusion.

Simultaneous to the lost child search that combed the hills, there was a check on all known degenerates. Anyone convicted of sex crimes had to prove an alibi to be cleared of suspicion. There were between 15 and 25 convicted sex offenders in San Diego then, and the city had a population of about 175,000. The town was still small enough that the authorities might be informed if someone suddenly skipped town and some of these suspects would not be cleared for a year or more.

Some 200 hundred Boy Scouts scoured the hills searching through the "thick underbrush and heavy growth of sage and chaparral on the hillsides." They could take a more detailed look and were welcomed as additional manpower. Indeed, in 1937 it would be the Boy Scouts that found the bodies of the two missing Everett sisters and the Stephens girl in a deep ravine after other searchers had scoured the surface above.

As the situation looked more dire, San Diego Chief of Police Hill broadened the search. The hills for miles around the Brooks home were searched. Every available man was involved. Over a thousand volunteers did their part. Planes from a nearby flight school circled overhead hoping for a glimpse of her red coat. Authorities at the nearby Mexican border were vigilant and a picture of Virginia was delivered to every police department and sheriff's office in the southwestern states.

The superintendent of a road crew reported he saw a girl that matched Virginia's description 35 miles east of San Diego at the Viejas grade. This sighting is probably one reason there was a concentrated search as far as Oklahoma. At about the same time, a local businessman added to the reward total.

"I have a family of my own and I know how my wife and I would feel were we to have an experience similar to that of Mr. and Mrs. Brooks. I prefer that my name not be mentioned. I am not seeking publicity. All I want to do is see that justice is done." The reward totaled $900 now. Enough to buy a brand new high-class car.

Two men of "low mentality" were taken in for questioning. A man of about 30 years of age was twice seen on the day Virginia disappeared with a girl answering Virginia's description. These leads had to be followed. The authorities never knew which one might break the case.

A deputy sheriff reported there was a sighting of Virginia in an automobile in the San Diego districts of El Cajon and Grossmont. The man was holding the girl "very close" on both occasions.

This sighting could be as innocent as a loving father and daughter, as potentially normal as the sighting in front of the store when the man bought the newspaper and the little girl could have been crying because he wouldn't buy her candy. Both of these scenarios are as typical as everyday life itself, but they had to be checked. For all anyone knew, the little girl in each case could have been Virginia.

A.S. Changnon, a lemon grower, said he saw a girl the Thursday or Friday following Virginia's disappearance acting oddly near the edge of the pond in San Diego. Footprints there were consistent with Virginia's footprints of shoes found near her house. They dragged the lake and were probably relieved when they didn't find anything. There was still hope. Another sighting was of a girl with a middle-aged man in the "rugged, brush-covered Broadway extension district" the day after she disappeared. Detectives found footprints there and they again matched the footprints her shoes made near her home previously, but that was evidently a common shoe. A coat was also found by the Espee (Southern Pacific) Tracks. Children are notorious for losing coats when outside playing hard because they may get warm enough to take them off. Like the other leads, it had to be followed, especially if it was a red coat with a fur collar.

Mrs. Irwin S. Martin of 4975 Trojan Avenue reported she saw Virginia with a man at 8:30 Wednesday morning. The girl did not look frightened and she was carrying a coat on one arm and books under the other arm. This was near the short cut Virginia frequently took on her way to school, but that address is a block north of Orange Ave, and Euclid School is at the intersection of Orange Ave. and Euclid Street. Perhaps Mrs. Martin saw the pair elsewhere and exactly where Virginia's shortcut was is not specified. Maps and street names are too different today to make a good guess. If that was Virginia so close to the school, why didn't she meet her friend Katie Lucero?

A coat was found as far away as Little Tujunga on the rocks of the wash in San Fernando, north of Los

Angeles. Virginia had been missing for 7 days and the coat looked like it had been there for several days. The woman who found it turned it over to the Valley division of the LAPD and a "large posse" searched the area because the coat tallied with the one Virginia wore. As it turned out, it could not have been the same coat since Virginia's was still with her body when it was discovered.

J.B. Tracy of Los Angeles reported he saw Virginia with a man who matched the description of Frank Lindsay, who escaped from the Washington State Prison. The case was complicated by the fact he took his 11-year-old step-daughter, Pearl, with him after he buried her mother in their backyard. That of course raised multiple alarms.

Tracy told police the man was light-haired and the girl he identified as Virginia looked drugged. Although he saw the man and girl in a battered sedan on Friday, three days after she disappeared, he did not see Virginia's picture in the paper until the following Sunday, and didn't report it until then.

Everett Frank Lindsay was "wanted for two murders, forgery, bigamy, army desertion and the abduction of two young girls." It is not clear if the two young girls were Pearl and Virginia or not. There were some reports he was wanted for "attacking four small girls in Seattle and Napa."

Pearl was found in Oakland and brought to Los Angeles. Lindsay eluded police there and was reported to be headed to the Imperial Valley east of San Diego and this would likely be another reason the search went east. But if he had Virginia, wouldn't Pearl say so?

Little Katie Lucero herself became a complication. She was adopted and there was speculation the kidnappers meant to kidnap her for ransom. But that was only a theory. More confusing, Mrs. D.M. Carder told police she was certain she saw Virginia and other children playing near a culvert. She was sure Katie was one of them. Katie denied that she had seen Virginia at all on the fateful day and said she did not go near the culvert because her father threatened to spank her if he found her near the place. As the Joplin Globe reported on Feb. 15:

"Katie told several stories which later proved to be falsehoods and was repeatedly coached by her mother in Mexican."

Police dragged the creek at the culvert thinking Katie may have fallen in and the children were afraid to say so out of fear of being punished.
That possibility is not so far-fetched. Two young schoolgirls ditched school during this time period and were feared kidnapped until they were found playing in a ravine. They feared punishment due to bad grades.

Also under suspicion was a "gang of young hoodlums" that hung out in Descanso and were said to be going to Arizona. So that was another reason the search was "extended across the border mountains, through Imperial Valley and into Arizona."

In Pasadena, police found blood soaked children's clothing in the yard of the McKinley-street school. They were various sizes of dresses, pajamas and other types of clothing and despite the size discrepancy they had to be looked at in a possible connection to Virginia.

Was it human blood? A practical joke? Alarming reports like this were not necessarily followed up unless a connection to Virginia was found, and it never was. It is enough to incite speculation.

The reward was up to $1,400, enough to buy 2 new cars in 1931 enough for a good down payment on a house, given that the average cost was $6,790.00.

One promising lead was the clue found by Long Beach police near Los Angeles. A man with a girl thought to be Virginia was observed by an officer when the man used a fictitious name and address when he bought a car. Was this connected to the man who bought a car in San Diego and then went to Pomona, abandoning his home there?

In El Centro, CA, 110 miles east of Virginia's home, there was an attempt to kidnap a 10-year-old girl. A "red headed woman" called at one of the El Centro grammar schools and asked for one of the children, saying the child's mother was ill and wanted her. She left when the child went to get her sister from another class and investigation revealed the mother was not sick. The woman was traced, police said, to the Filipino section. This woman was arrested and charged with attempted kidnapping of little Helen Alex, the 10-year-old Imperial Valley schoolgirl.

Along about the same time police were investigating the disappearance of a girl from Brawley and another from Holtville. Fortunately, these cases were not severe enough to make headlines.

A wife reported her husband missing when he disappeared from San Diego the same day Virginia disappeared. His name was Roche. There is no further mention of him in this context in the newspapers.

Brig. Gen. Robert McCleave from Fort Rosecrans offered some of his troops to help search and drag pools.

There was a sighting as far north as Portland, Ore., and that had to be followed. Did someone Virginia knew in Portland have her? The search east encompassed Arizona, New Mexico and Texas. Deputy Sheriff Blake Mason enlisted the aid of officers as far east as Amarillo, Texas. On the 19th of

Feb. Mason telegraphed from Phoenix that a girl identified by photographs as Virginia had stopped at Wellton, Arz. for two days with a man about 50 years old who "posed as her father." "Thin, tall, wearing a small mustache and glasses. The girl wore knickers, golf stockings and tan Oxford shoes." Deputy Mason directed the Arizona phase of the search, which extended over the entire West and he thought Virginia had been kidnaped. [Correct spelling back then.]

"A girl resembling Virginia was seen at Tacna and Wellton, in Southwestern Arizona, over the weekend. "It is possible that she and her kidnaper are hiding in Phoenix," Mason reported. Four people informed Mason they saw a child resembling Virginia in the Wellton district where many tourists were held up by a flood which occurred Friday night when a retaining wall back of the town gave way. "These people said the girl was accompanied by an elderly man. We have clues pertaining to that man but they are not being made public just yet," Mason added. The search included Northern Arizona and along New Mexico in the event the kidnapper evaded Southern Arizona officers who started hunting the previous Monday. Mexico was also a possibility since Wellton was only a few miles from an isolated section of the international border.

On the 20th of Feburary, Fred A. Kenny, Sheriff,

notified Mason that a middle aged man and a girl resembling Virginia stopped over night at a Tombstone auto camp about two days previously. San Diego officers began a search at Nogales, Ariz, where the middle aged man and the girl were reported seen. Deputy Mason hurried to the border town. Mason telephoned headquarters from Nogales and informed his superiors he had no luck. He planned to follow a lead that the girl was seen in Phoenix. On the 21st, 11 days after she disappeared, the search continued over several states. Deputy Mason reported the middle aged man and the girl had "back tracked" toward to Phoenix and he planned to catch up to them within 24 hours.

A garage attendant who filled their gas tank said the older man and the girl were in a Ford coupe and the girl's coat was thrown over the back of the seat. The search continued into "Tia Juna," Mexicali and other towns on the Mexican border and all over the Imperial Valley.

A man was arrested in El Paso, Texas on Feb. 19th because he drove a green Ford coupe. He did not have a child with him.

Escondido is about 30 miles north of San Diego and from there Sheriff Carl Klindt reported a sighting by two men of an automobile driven by a man who was seen with a girl resembling Virginia Brooks near San Marcos. The girl was peering from a window of a green Ford coupe. The driver was a man about 50 years old traveling with the girl on a little used highway; the girl was wrapped in a blanket. The driver sat on her feet. As the coupe sped away, they saw the girl raise her head and she gave the two men a frightened glance. The men identified the girl even to a broken tooth distinguishing the Brooks child. The two Escondido merchants, unnamed at first, told Klindt the car passed once and the man was sitting on the girl's feet, holding her down with his hands. The second time the car passed, the merchants' car was stuck in the mud on a narrow road. They tried to flag down the car for help but it sped up and passed them. Both times the man was holding the girl down in the seat.

It is possible the girl in the car was frightened of the two men because the man driving, whatever his relation to the girl, spoke of not wanting to stop for strangers on a desolate road. Her response might be a look of fear. Why he was holding her down is another question, and readers of mystery might have some ideas. We will come back to these two merchants because, as one reporter describes it, they are witnesses in the "long arm of coincidence." Perhaps that long arm is so long it stretches credibility.

Possibly the most intriguing turn of events started out as a report that Virginia was seen in a car with a man. An unidentified informant reported to Undersheriff Dewar that he saw Virginia in a car on

Fortieth Street in Los Angeles and supplied the license plate number. That plate registration led them to a house in Pomona that was probably abandoned days before. Neighbors said they hadn't seen the occupant since the previous Friday and they never saw anyone with him. A careful search of the house turned up a photograph of the man they were seeking as the driver of the car, and --strangely enough--a photograph of Virginia's father. John Brooks said he did not know the man and did not know why he would have a photo of him. Deputies Cloud and Alres learned the man had driven to San Diego the previous week from Pomona, and while there traded his automobile in on another, asserting he was about to make a hurried trip to Arizona. Another man was supposedly with him. The officers somehow traced the man back to Torrance where they learned he was supposed to be on his mining claim and had left for his mine in Lebec, at the northern Los Angeles County line on the ridge route north of Saugus. Because the man claimed he was going to drive to Arizona, one search concentrated on the northern deserts of the State, with roadblocks in the entire Southwest. This was yet another reason to think a man was taking Virginia east.

Deputy Mason linked this information with the sighting of the girl and her abductor when they stopped for two days the previous week near Tacne, Ariz., during the flood. Meanwhile, authorities in San

Diego and Los Angeles thought they had their man and he was said to be at his mine in Lebec.

The newspapers reported this as a massive manhunt that would result in the arrest of Virginia's abductor in the mountains above Los Angeles. A swarm of law enforcement surrounded the mine ready to make the arrest. The man convinced the authorities the woman with him was his wife, not a young girl.

Mrs. Matilda Litman reported a sighting including the details that she gave a ride to a middle-aged man and a small girl the previous Sunday on the outskirts of Los Angeles. When she saw the picture of Virginia she noticed a resemblance.

Mrs. Litman got a threatening letter for her trouble:

"Mrs. Mathilda Litman: It took you a long time to get your name in the papers didn't it? If this case in regards to this poor little girl didn't happen you would get your nose in some other case anyway. Wash your dirty clothes at home and you will have all you can tend to. You and all like you are nothing but that wind on the street won't blow by. Look out."

The police gave her neighborhood extra patrols. John Bitnoff was thought kidnaped by two Filipinos after he left school on Feb. 19th. He was offered a ride by them in their blue sedan.

He is not in the paper after February 21, so he

was likely found safe and sound.

Mr. S.A. Nichols, 17400 Oakview Drive, reported seeing Virginia in a battered small coupe with two Mexicans on North Sepulveda Boulevard in the San Fernando Valley. Acting Lieutenant Berger took the report that she and her chauffeur, Will Haas, saw the girl the morning before while out for a drive. The girl appeared to be "extremely frightened and she was swathed in a blanket while sitting between the two young Mexicans. Later that night Lieut. Berger showed Mrs. Nichols a picture of the missing girl. "I know that is the girl I saw," she said.

Two men said they gave a man and girl resembling Virginia a ride from Saugus to Tulare. They said they were bound for Oakland and told police the child said she was 10 and had not seen her mother for days. William P. Bond, 1203 North Meyers Street, Burbank, and T.J. Shaheen 1075 Queen Ann Road, West Inglewood, N.J., were the men, and they said the girl was acting cowed and fearful, refusing to tell her name.

The man with her was unusually reticent. When they stopped to eat at a roadside restaurant, Bond and Shaheen explained they were unable to induce the man to enter the restaurant, but they were finally able to persuade the child. She ate lightly while the man remained outside. At Tulare, the men said the man insisted on leaving and they attempted to give him money to pay railroad fare for himself and the girl, but the man wouldn't have it. Officers immediately checked on the report along with the many other scattered reports of having seen the child.

William J. Snow, 50, was held in the Brooks kidnapping case. Snow applied to a boarding house proprietor for lodging for his "little niece, whose mother died in Portland, Ore., recently." Under police questioning, he said he spoke of an imaginary niece for his own amusement. In another article, it was thought Snow sought the help for child care and spoke in detail with various people who advertised their services, but he never appeared with a child. Snow was traced through one of the housewives in a small Hollywood hotel. He was held due to bounced check he wrote for a room. Snow was cleared just a few hours after his arrest when he was able to prove he was in Los Angeles when Virginia Brooks disappeared. He was still held on a forgery charge.

There was a growing fear as the futile search warned of a foreboding outcome: "We have run down every available bit of information and have searched widely without success," Chief of Police Hill said, "and while we remain vigorous as ever in the search we cannot but fear that nothing will develop."

In Ventura, a man and a child rented a room in a Ventura hotel one night and they were reportedly acting suspiciously. A child's coat left behind was thought to be Virginia's.

There were reports that a middle aged man and girl were seen crossing the Mexican border and they would be apprehended within 24 hours.

Sheriff at Haskell, Tex., W.T. Sarrels reported that as a matter of fact the man and girl were seen in Haskell. "Parties seen here yesterday" was the statement of the telegraph from Sarrels. "Man wearing blue serge suit, white hat. Man about 5'10" or 11"; shaved; some gray at temples. Girl about 10, brown hair, blue eyes. Driving a 1930 Ford coach with California license. Try Oklahoma City" So the telegram ended.

L. Kirkbride, a clerk and Charles McHugh, bellboy at Fifth and Los Angeles street hotel, were sure a man of about 60 who described himself as James Croad of Buffalo, N.Y., registered at the hotel on Sunday, and had Virginia. The man said he and the girl had just motored from Arizona. They stayed the night and it was unknown where they were going.

A fourth clew failed when Deputy Sheriff Mason found no trace of the man and child he was seeking. A jeweler's tip of the man with a girl trying to hock a watch could not be tracked down to specific persons.

Hope was fading after nine days of her being missing. There were reports of sightings seen in Long Beach, Wellton, Ariz., Wichita, Kans, and numerous other places, but no concrete evidence was found. The search of the canyons and brush "east of the city" and the questioning of friends, motorists, relatives and schoolmates failed to offer anything concrete. Adding insult to injury, Virginia's parents vigorously denied a rumor that Virginia was a child by a former marriage. They produced hospital records from Indianapolis, Ind. where Virginia was born. Hope was beginning to fade despite the widespread manhunt over the entire Southwest.

There were no solid leads until the tragic find one month after she disappeared, and when her body was found, John Brooks said what many felt: "I could tear his heart out!"

Fear Missing Coast Girl Slain

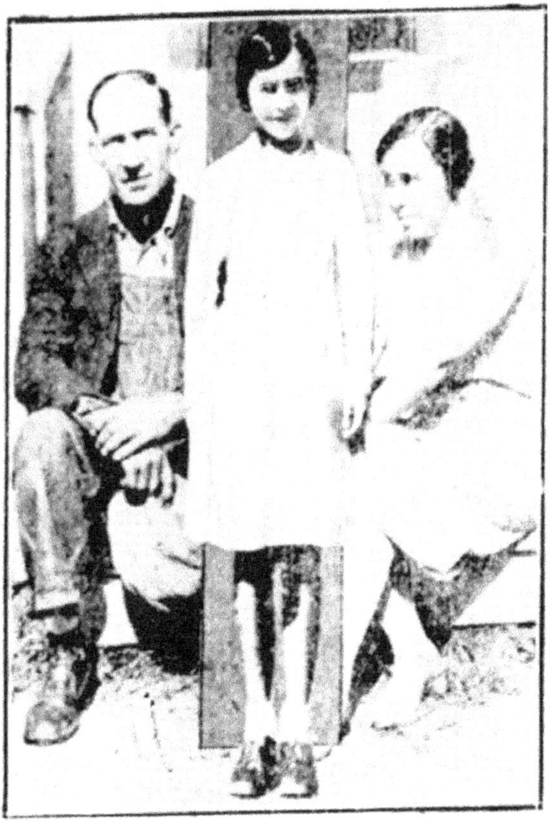

Brush covered hills near San [illegible] Los Angeles, Cal., are being searched by scores of [illegible] for trace of the missing Virginia [illegible] San Diego girl, feared the victim of a [illegible]. The girl has been mysteriously missing since February [illegible] Los Angeles. In the photo, Mr. and Mrs. [illegible] are shown.

Figure 4 Virginia's aunt’s pictures were used for the investigation.

Chapter 4: Tragic Find

Her body was found in an old gunnysack about 14 miles north of San Diego on the Camp Kearney Mesa. Another gunnysack containing her books was found nearby. Like my other two books, these facts will be detailed in the hopes of inciting interest by experts in forensic psychology and forensic science. The profile of this killer, for example, would probably not be one of the disorganized killer. That is because he did not leave the body where the murder happened and he did not leave the weapon at that crime scene. Nor were there any fingerprints on the library books Virginia checked out, not even her own prints. This was similar to the lack of prints on the shoes neatly lined in a row in the 1937 case, as they did not have any prints on them either. This suggests a more organized killer. The initial reports were that Virginia Brooks' body was dismembered. It was thought she was beheaded.

In this chapter the focus is on the suspect list in

terms of murder, which changed the dynamics not only in relation to police effort but also in terms of the type of criminal. The next chapter will concentrate on the forensic evidence, of which there was a surprising amount and an equally surprising understanding of it. Investigations were not as primitive as might be expected.

According to some reports, "Blackie" the collie was attracted to the burlap gunny sack and pawed at it and barked. She ran back to her people with a "let me show you" bark, and then ran back to the gunnysack. Every dog owner has seen something similar.

George Moses was a goat herder on the mesa, and he walked this route daily. There was nothing else around to speak of but his goats lived on the mesa and so did he, and so did Blackie. He poked and prodded the gunnysack a little. His curiosity naturally raised he slit it open. As Moses told it, his dog's name was "Shep":

"I was out there herding sheep for Bert Vasey," said Moses. "Early yesterday morning my black dog Shep ran into a little clearing where I had shot at some birds last Friday.

"Shep found a gunnysack and made a big fuss over it. I went to investigate.

"With my knife I slashed a hole in the sack and

out rolled a child's skull.

"It was horrible. I didn't wait to investigate further, but ran to the road a mile away.

"A truck driver came along and I told him to notify the sheriff that I found a child's body on the mesa. The deputies came out and took the body.

"That's all I know.

"I never was so surprised and frightened in my life."

While waiting Moses stood guard over the evidence.

Deputy Sheriffs Mason, Tillery and Macumber, along with Chief of Police Hill, responded to the mesa. Reporters were quickly on the scene. The little red coat like the one Virginia wore was plainly visible. "Producing a scrap of cloth which he carried with him, a piece of red and brown plaid material which had come from the coat that Virginia had worn, Mason compared it with the coat which covered the skeleton-like form and declared that at last Virginia Brooks had been found." The skull was clear of hair and skin, leading some to think it was put in lime or some chemical. The red coat along with the library books were strong indications of a positive identification of Virginia Brooks.

Coroner Gunn arrived soon and removed the body to Goodbody's mortuary.

During the inquest, Virginia's mother testified

she would not accept that it was Virginia until later, and at the inquest she testified it was the chipped tooth mortician Goodbody showed her that finally overcame her denial.

Yes, it was Virginia. "I have never been satisfied that my little girl was really dead. That tooth, though, convinced me of the terrible reality of the whole thing," she testified.

The Coroner's jury rendered an "open verdict that she came to her death at the hands of a party or parties unknown.'" The 10 witnesses at the inquest: Mrs. Blanche M. Brooks, mother, John, F. Brooks, father; Gordon, her 12-year-old brother; Mrs. Lea Ward and W.E. Bell, who believe they are the last except her killer to see the child alive. George Moses, goat herder, the autopsy surgeon, police officers and deputy sheriffs.

Funeral services would be held March 21st with the grave site donated by Mayor Clark on behalf of the city. Mr. Goodbody donated the casket.

Not only was a little girl killed, but she was mutilated like Marion Parker, some newspapers claimed. Not only was she killed by a degenerate, but only the worst kind of criminal degenerate would do such a thing to a helpless child. The police of course refocused their investigations on the suspects closest to the scene of the crime, the ones who were in San Diego all along. The newspapers and the authorities picked up the drum beat with a fervor. The police set their sights on the man who "had a wicked gleam in his eye" and who lived in the vicinity of the crime. L.C. Odell, furniture dealer, and Bill Williams, trapper of mountain lions, were the two men that reported having seen a car pass them twice with a little girl in it wrapped in the blanket. On the second passing they were stuck in the mud and tried to flag the car down, but the driver of the old blue Ford accelerated past them. The two men now reported they gave the same man a ride to San Diego and throughout the ride the man ranted about the missing Brooks girl. After they let this mysterious man out downtown, the two men realized there was something familiar about the man.

"We let him out downtown," Williams stated. "He said he had been out of work for a long time, and had been living in a small shack and had just sold his car and was looking for a job. All the way into town we felt there was something familiar about the man. After he had left us, it occurred to us that he looked exactly like the man we had seen with the girl in that Ford three weeks ago."

Police called in reinforcements and combed the hills a few miles north of the Camp Kearney mesa in search of the mystery man's secluded home. Odell and Williams said the mean looking man had the demeanor of the moron. Kenneth O'Hara, the writer of the LA Times story, called these sightings the "long arm of coincidence."

Six men were under "strict surveillance" while previous suspects were released. Harry Wahlstrom, 28, was held after the body was found. He was a chicken rancher that some children accused of untoward conduct. He was in fact on probation for such a crime although it is not exactly clear what the conduct was. However, he was somehow able to establish his innocence through an alibi and the fact his hair did not match the hair found clutched in Virginia's fist. It helped when it was determined suspicious blood on the tree stump at his chicken ranch was chicken blood.

Another man was picked up the day the body was found but was released.

A man that committed suicide in a Los Angeles motel registered under George Silvers, transient. There was an envelope addressed to George H. Stout, Birmingham, Ala. The man had brown hair, was about 28, 5' 11", 165 lbs. "He had obliterated his name on a wallet and key ring." The suicide was investigated because he had newspaper stories opened in his room of Virginia's body being found. The police evidently had considered his suicide a potential expression of guilt, but it was also possible a murdered child was so depressing it put him over the edge. A sample of his dark brown hair was sent to San Diego and added to the list of hair samples Welch would have to compare.

A library card in one of the books indicated they were due on the 11th and Virginia must have planned to return them after school. It is not clear if the police considered her trying to return them that morning, but they must have looked into it. One article states the volume of poems included "Just because I Ate That Apple Pie," "The Birthplace of Jesus," and "Daddy's Got a New Car". Most articles consistently listed other books.

The books found in the other gunnysack were "Real Story Book," by Wadsworth; "Listen to me Stories," by Alicia Aspinwall; a third "Johnny Crowe's Garden," by Brooks, and the fourth "About Harriet," by Hunt.

"Real Story Book" was published in 1927 and it consists of classic stories retold by Wallace Wadsworth: "Peter Rabbit," "The gingerbread man," "The three bears," "Little black Sambo," "The pied piper," for a total of 20 children's stories in 126 pages. The rich illustrations are by Margaret Evans Price, whose husband, Irving Price, founded the Fisher-Price toy company with his partners.

Dutton published Mrs. Alicia Aspinwall's "Listen to me Stories" in 1910, and the contents consisted of "The echo-maid," "In the land of the wee-uns," "The big light on Burning Mountain," "A leap-year boy," "A discontented rooster" and "The box-eating antarilla."

Google images returns many hits of outstanding artwork with a search of "Johnny Crow's Garden," written and illustrated by L. Leslie Brooks (1903). Virginia, no relation, apparently loved illustrated books and this one is exceptional.

"About Harriet" by Clara Whitehill Hunt was published in 1916 and the ebook is available at Goggle Books. The seven stories about a 4-year-old girl are "What she did on Friday, "What she did on Saturday," "What she did on Sunday, "What she did on Monday," "What she did on Tuesday, "What she did on Wednesday" and the 7th is, "What she did on Thursday."

Of course, everyone wanted to know what Virginia Brooks did on Wednesday, February 11 and how soil and mold got on some of the pages of the books and how she died.

If she did try to drop them in the library box that morning, she would have to walk 16 blocks past Euclid to the East San Diego Library at 4085 Fairmount Ave. (Thanks to Derek Moses of the San Diego Public Library for that surprisingly difficult to confirm address.) The blocks were very short, however, because the developer thought corners more valuable, so perhaps it was 8 normal blocks. Even with short blocks, that would add a half mile and an additional 10 minutes each way. But why wouldn't Katie Lucero see her? Did Virginia tell Katie she had to go the library and Katie forgot? Would that explain the sighting of her walking with a man? More likely, the police checked this angle and it didn't pan out.

Undersheriff Oliver Sexson thought Virginia would not get into a car with a total stranger and therefore she knew the fiend. "In many of its details the case is a striking parallel in the mystery murder late in 1927 of Nicholas Esperaza, 13-year-old Mexican boy. He disappeared under similar circumstance and several months later his corpse was found by a hunter at a spot about three miles from where Virginia's body was discovered. Gordon Stewart Northcott later made a partial confession of this crime, but, given under pressure of questioning, it was discarded as a fabrication." [1]

On March 14, The LA Times printed an article titled "BROOKS MURDER SEARCH SPURRED."

Mr. and Mrs. John Brooks, parents of Virginia Brooks, 10-yearold girl, whose decapitated body was found last Tuesday on the Camp Kearny Mesa, today emerged from seclusion and made a personal request that police question a youth they believe may have committed the appalling crime. The broken-hearted

---

[1] This is the same Northcott that was the serial killer depicted in the movie "Changeling," staring Angelina Jolie and directed by Clint Eastwood.

couple visited the police substation in East San Diego and presented the request to detectives investigating leads in that vicinity. They asked that the recent movements of a certain youth who lives in the general direction of their own home be checked thoroughly and reported on, in order that their suspicions may be either confirmed or dispelled.,

NAME WITHHELD This youth, whose name is withheld, but who is said to be the son of wealthy parents, was brought to the attention of Mr. and Mrs. Brooks, they told the officers, by the mother of a girl about Virginia's age. Their informant told them her daughter about a year ago had complained of unwelcome attentions on the part of the youth involved. "We cannot make a direct accusation against this young man," Mrs. Brooks told the detectives, "but we will feel relieved if you can assure that he had no hand in this terrible thing. The mother of this other little girl, through the story she told us about him, has fixed him in our minds as the possible perpetrator of Virginia's murder." A detail of detectives set out at once in search of the suspected youth, but at a late hour tonight had not apprehended him for questioning.

What, exactly the investigation uncovered about this young man, if anything, was never reported in the news, except that he was cleared. There may still be details in the cold case files of the authorities, but the young man was obviously not convicted of this crime.

At the request of San Diego police, a driver of a bungalow-on-wheels, or what we might call a camper or motor home today, became a factor when dispatches from El Centro, east of San Diego and near the Mexican border, reported the arrest of Herbert Ogelsby, 56, a homesteader of the lakeside district nearby. Ogelsby, according to the information received by local investigators, left San Diego about the middle of February, traveling in "bungalowautomobile" which contained a secret compartment. Circumstances involving the driver as a suspect were not revealed, but leaving San Diego was suspicious enough. He was absolved of all suspicion when he established that on the day Virginia was kidnaped, he was in El Centro. The Tax Collector there supported his statement that he had applied for a job as a house painter.

When M. F. Nuremberg, expert criminologist attached to the State bureau of criminal investigation, arrived, there was new hope by the public that the case could quickly be solved. Nuremberg and Chief of Police Hill had a private review of all of the evidence as Nuremberg was brought up to speed on the details. After, accompanied by Detective Sergeant Berg, he visited the Brooks home and conferred with Mr. and Mrs. Brooks. All they could tell him was that Virginia started for school on the morning of February 11. That Mrs. Brooks watched her disappear around a bend in University Avenue and they never saw her again or learned her fate until the body was found on the mesa. There is an uncanny similarity here to the murder of Geneva Hardman in 1920 Kentucky. That tragedy is depicted in screenplay format in *Lynch Him!*

Tips from citizens had always been plentiful since Virginia disappeared. The mounting rewards contributed to the effort. As we've seen, there were so many leads it stretched the investigation thin despite all the support from other jurisdictions. Mr. and Mrs. A. T. Moffett of Altadena spent a day with deputy sheriffs going over the mesa where the body was found and offering their assistance in tracking down clews. This could be in response to the sightings by L.C. Odell, furniture dealer, and Bill Williams, trapper of mountain lions. Mrs. Moffett was a sister of the slain girl's mother, a different aunt than the one who supplied the photos. She reported a vague clue of having seen a mysterious man frequently in the Brooks neighborhood for some time before the girl vanished. On many occasions, she said, he strolled up and down the road in front of the Brooks home, especially after Virginia had returned from school. She was able to provide a good description of the stranger but no hint of his identity or present whereabouts. He stopped coming there, she stated, the day the girl disappeared. There was investigation of the Brooks neighbors without result.

Clues like this raise more questions. If Mrs. Moffett lived in Altadena, over 3 miles from Virginia's home, how often did she visit? Did the police canvass Virginia's neighborhood and Mrs. Moffett could not provide an identification that would solve the case? Did all with a similar description have alibis? Answering these questions would be time consuming and require manpower, but law enforcement undoubtedly followed every lead and excluded similar looking neighbors, if any.

Detective Captain Paul Hayes received a letter claiming voodoo rituals were to blame for the girl's murder. Without revealing the name of the author, Capt. Hayes explained the letter argued the theory Virginia was "offered up as a sacrifice on the altar of a black magic cult. He charged also that the murder of little Nicholas Esparza, whose body was found on the Camp Kearny mesa in 1927, was the work of the same weird cult." Capt. Hayes "conferred" with the letter writer seeking more solid clues and in the end did not see a reliable connection to the case.

One of the strangest leads was that of Jerry L. Davis, 21, who was a "graduate of four reformatories." He came under suspicion when charged for a burglary, by some accounts and a robbery in others, he wanted to quickly plead guilty and get sent to San Quentin for life, where he would be safe. He offered vague suggestions that he committed some major crime and going to Quentin would save his life. Police wondered if that crime was the murder of Virginia Brooks. Did he think he would escape suspicion if he was doing a life sentence? Did he want to do life as a form of punishment for killing Virginia? In direct contradiction, Davis consistently denied knowing anything about the Brooks case and claimed to have no part in it. Whatever he did, the police all over the state were more than willing to follow every lead. A sample of his hair must not have matched the hair found in Virginia's clutched fist.

Authorities all the way to Oklahoma were cooperating in the Brooks case. California authorities requested detention of Joe Davidson, alias Gerald Davidson, for "comparison of his Bertillon measurement and general description." Bertillon measurements might be compared to facial recognition measurements today, except specific body parts were measured on the theory that each body differs in the same way fingerprints differ. This theory was widely accepted without reservation until 1903, when a Bertillon match of Will West matched William West. The newly arriving prisoner in Leavenworth denied having been there before, despite the Bertillon match. Since the prisoner he matched was already in the same prison, he was obviously telling the truth. The fingerprints did match for Davidson, however, and they were of Gerald Dorsei (another spelling?) California authorities came to believe Dorsei was not involved in the Brooks case. He was freed then immediately rearrested at the telegrammed request of California authorities, probably CII, though never extradited to California.

When arrested in Oklahoma Dorsei had a bloodstained shirt and female clothing in his possession, and had previously been arrested for annoying a small girl. He willingly admitted to leaving Fresno, CA, soon after Virginia vanished, but denied any part of the crime. Fresno is almost 400 miles north of San Diego. He was cleared to the satisfaction of California authorities.

Reports of suspicious characters flooded police all over the state. Citizens were activated and vigilant. A mutilator of little girls was on the prowl and everyone wanted him caught before it was too late for another child. Reports to the police more than doubled, the LA Times reported.

"Herbert Oglesby, 56 years of age, was arrested [in El Centro] this afternoon by Police Chief Frank P. McCaslin at 'the request of San Diego officers who advised that he is wanted for investigation in connection with the death of Virginia Brooks. Oglesby is held in the County Jail awaiting the arrival of San Diego officers. McCaslin reported that he found on the man's bed an old San Diego newspaper containing pictures of the Brooks family, and a stack of detective magazines, with a page turned at a story relating to "snaring love nest murderers."

Given that evidence, the suspect pool could expand to everyone who read the news stories about the missing child.

Another article by Kenneth O'Hara for LA Times, March 15, explained another arrest:

"The long arm of the law reached into Mexico today and brought back a new suspect in its relentless search for the murderer of little Virginia Brooks. He is held in jail here tonight under the name of Ture Wallin, pending further investigation of his movements during the past month or so. Wallin was taken in custody at Tecate by Deputy Sheriffs Mason and Buck and Detectives Osborne and Shea on word from Tecate authorities that he has been garrulous recently in regard to the baffling crime. The officers here say preliminary check-up shows he disappeared from San Diego shortly after the Brooks girl vanished while on her way to school February 11, adding he owns a Ford coupe similar to the car reported to have been seen parked at the curbing near the Brooks home on that date. Technically, Wallin, a Swedish fisherman, was booked for investigation by immigration authorities and for assertedly jumping a bond given here some time ago on a traffic violation charge."

He was released after police decided the 28-year-old fisherman just talked too much.

Some good news was heard when a home-sic 10-year-old girl returned home safely after she runaway back to San Diego where her friends were. She and her family moved to Venice Beach and those hundreds of miles were evidently too far from her friends in San Diego. Her name was Wanda Downs and she may not have thought it a 100% happy ending, but she lived to adjust. Everyone else was 100% happy about that.

Neal Marsh, on March, 31, became a new suspect. He had lodgings at Sixteenth and K Streets. "Marsh completed a sixty-day sentence in the San Diego County Jail on January 31 for attempting to strangle a Coronado woman. He was dishonorably discharged and in 1923 was on probation for robbing the Oakland National Guard armory. He did two years in prison for grand theft. He was cleared of the Brooks case.

While it may be possible some police departments were raising the stakes on any suspect for anything by using the Brooks murder, it is also possible they thought they never knew if someone in custody was in fact involved. If they knew then what we know now, they would have proceeded with the same doggedness with different eyes and a wider scope and they may have solved the case.

John Paul, 45, was held when a 10-year-old girl was rescued from his home. The cabbage grower lived at Thirty-Second Street and Island Avenue in San Diedo when Mrs. Madeline Butera, his neighbor, reported she knocked on Paul's door to buy cabbage and it took an unusual amount of time for him to answer. When he did, he seemed nervous. After informing Paul of her order he left her at the door to fetch the cabbages, and she saw a little girl peer anxiously from behind some curtains as she waited. Mrs. Butera immediately went to a nearby relative who had a phone and called police. Officers overpowered Paul after a rough and tumble at the back door as he tried to flee. The child was inside and she stated she had been attacked, which in the 1930s meant she was raped. Assistant Police Surgeon Crabtree substantiated it.

She was told he would give her a penny and some candy if she went to his house. He held her there for four hours before she was rescued. The "moral panic" the Brooks case inspired saved the little girl because Mrs. Butera had Virginia Brooks in mind when she saw the frightened child through the window.

A jury deliberated only twenty minutes before finding him guilty and he was sentenced to from 1 year to life in prison in May of 1931.

Paul reportedly would not answer questions regarding the Brooks case but the forensic evidence excluded him.

More than 4,000 people attended the funeral rites of little Virginia Brooks. There was only room for 500 of them inside the Mormon services at Rodgers mortuary in East San Diego. The other 3,500 stood outside in a show of support. Virginia's friends openly cried and weathered men wept. Virginia's father and brothers let tears escape their fond memories while her mother failed to hold back despite her stoic effort. Two women fainted and were cared for in the chapel anteroom. A duet of "Sometime We Shall Understand" was sang by two members of the Mormon quartet.

"There is brightness in all dark hours," said the Rev. Holtzinger, the pastor of Ashbury Methodist church where Virginia would sometimes attend Sunday school. "And brightness in this dark hour is to be found in the common sympathy of this community and nation which goes out to the Brooks family. A thing like this, a fatal thrust at the heart of a defenseless child, has made us united as one. May the officers seeking the doer of this deed have their efforts crowned with success. Not only may the guilty person be captured, but may there be speedy justice for the perpetrator of this horrible thing. The officers must prosecute their hunt for the slayer until he is found. The sanctity of our homes and children must be protected.

"'Suffer little children to come unto me and forbid them not, for of such is the kingdom of heaven'....

"It is comforting to know this little child is safe in the fold of the Shepherd's eternal care."

Law enforcement would be more comforted if while eying the service they got the perpetrator in their sights, but no such luck. If the killer was there, he did not reveal himself.

"Virginia has gone to the beyond, but her heart is turned toward us. The gates of heaven, where again she shall know her mother and loved ones, have been thrown open to this child, taken from us in her innocent youth," intoned the Reverend Mr. Tenney. The quartet sang hymns as the thousands filed through the chapel to view the white velour-covered casket of purity, flowers all around caressing it with their fragile lives.

Notes of Virginia's favorite song, "Let Us Speak Kind Words to One Another," that she often sang with her mother, drifted outside to the senses of the thousands present. Six of Virginia's classmates accepted the honor of being pallbearers of the white casket with the single rose laid on top. All six girls wore bob haircuts of varying lengths, possibly in memory of Virginia's shingle bob.

After a short service, the thousands lined up to watch the six classmates of Virginia's 5th grade class carry the casket of purity to the waiting hearse. All six girls perhaps played a part in the Norse Brunhilda presentation of a few months before, and they could have thought of themselves as little Valkyrie pallbearers honoring their betrayed friend.

The authorities did not give up, of course, and were still hard at work. If anything, the funeral with all it tearful glory reinvigorated their efforts. A "Mexican youth" who said he knew who killed the "little San Diego girl" and he "had to get something off my mind," Manuel Lopez surrendered to police in Los Angeles. He named an insurance collector and after investigation it was determined there were personal differences that motivated the accusation, which was not much more than hallucination. He was not detained.

In Santa Barbara, a man named Crashley, alias William O'Conner, 40, was arrested for attacking an 8-year-old girl. Undersheriff Jack Ross noted the suspect talked glibly about the Brooks crime, but denied any hand in it, maintaining he had obtained his information from newspapers.

Reid H. O'Brien, 21, made the mistake of having a bloody knife in his car along with a gun. He was arrested for the theft of several hundred dollars in postal money orders from his mother's store. Captain Bright questioned him and O'Brien explained that a friend bled on the car seat after an accident but he could not explain the bloody knife or the gun. His description was similar to the man Mrs. B.H. Ward described as being near Radio Road when the Brooks girl was approaching him. His mother's store/post office was in Tecate on the Mexican border in the mountains east of San Diego. He visited his friend, Ed Rouse, who lived at Fifth and Quince streets near Balboa Park; then he was arrested trying to cash a money order.

A man named Smith Harris sued for false arrest and claimed:

"All floaters, jobless transients who had neither money nor influence, were suspected. Harris, an out of work printer, went to San Diego seeking a job and found himself in the dragnet. He was arrested for "questioning". When he demanded legal counsel, he was slugged in the jaw. Legal rights, more blows, anyone who demanded their rights must have something to hide. He had a lot to say about it when he sued:

"They trussed me up and used a rubber hose. Although it is as brutal as a heavy leather quirt, the hose ordinarily leaves no mark to betray police methods "But the one they used on me had been lying in dirt, and the sand cut my back and left livid marks. After a few cuts with the hose my inquisitors stopped and began vigorously slapping the welts with their hands. This brought the blood to the surface and made the next series of slashes more painful. They repeated the beating and slapping five times. Then they placed my ear tips between thumbtacks. They squeezed the tack through but I didn't feel as much pain as I did from the hose beatings. The thumbtack torture, like the rubber hose, can't be detected. The holes heal speedily. They gave me one more beating and then they put me in a cell to think it over. I was promised another beating if the five hours of allotted thinking time should fail to loosen my tongue. But the worst was over. Police evidently decided they were on the wrong track. A sergeant said they had decided to release me, but before you go I'm going to give a memento to carry to your lawyer.' With that he blackened my left eye. The police let me go--I was innocent."

His lawsuit failed.

As the investigation turned into April, the LA Times reported this article:

NEW SUSPECT LOCATED

'San Diego Police Working on Clews Which Indicate Man as Virginia Brooks' Slayer

'(1) Failed to report to his usual work on the morning of February 11, the day Virginia was kidnaped.

'(2) That he was previously known to have attacked an 11-year-old child in the basement of his home.

'The suspect is in an institution in California and may be brought to San Diego for questioning. The man was already a suspect after the body was found. "Sheriff's officers investigating him at that time satisfied themselves that he had no connection with the case. However, in the light of recent developments, we will leave nothing undone to learn the suspect's every move prior to the time the child disappeared," Said Sears. The man was known to have traveled by the Brooks home every day on his way to work and he probably passed shortly before 8 a.m. the morning the child was kidnaped.'

As promising as that lead sounds, it led nowhere. If he did not have access to gunnysacks and molded leaves, or his hair did not match the hair found under Virginia's fingernails, and he did not have access to a vehicle that could leave the tire tracks found at the crime scene, and if he did not match any of the descriptions witnesses offered, and for other reasons known only to the authorities, he was excluded as a suspect.

As possible suspects were excluded, those who remained as viable possible perpetrators thinned. News reports of March 28 stated the list was narrowed down to only 3 suspects remaining. These three lived near Virginia's home and were under constant surveillance.

After the news reports that the list of suspects was whittled down to three, Lieut. Sears waved a list of pages of 300 names and addresses in the air of his office. Everyone on it was a suspect or was, he pointed out. The majority was eliminated but there was still a long list. "Published reports that we have shaved the long list of suspect in the Brooks case down to three are incorrect," Sears said. "Look at this list. Every person whose name appears here is a suspect, or was a suspect. Of these here we have eliminated the greater part. But the claim we have only three suspects in mind at present is wrong."

However, undisclosed sources said otherwise, saying the total current list could be counted on one hand. So few they could keep them under surveillance at all times. If they were not the guilty ones, then those in the know suspected the child killer might never be caught.

Richard Ward, 56, an escaped Folsom convict and murderer had a mountain home shack for 10 years. "I never hurt anybody unless they hurt me first," Ward said. He had been sentenced twice for murder. His claimed name, John "Jack" McVane, was an alias. Another suspect, Asher Williams, 50, was a confessed assailant of small girls. He was in L.A. County Jail for attacking a 4-year-old girl. He broke down under questioning and said, "I am unable to trust myself around young girls." He wanted help in a state institution, he said. The witnesses who said they saw a man with Virginia while she walked to school failed to identify Williams as the man or even someone similar. "We are convinced that the slayer of Virginia Brooks was the same type as Williams but we have been unable to show that Williams even knew the Brooks girl," said Capt. Hickok of the BII.

Merle Mercer, 25, with a long record of burglary and robbery also became a suspect. All three were cleared.

Were these the last three suspects the media reported as being the final possibilities? The San Diego authorities undoubtedly did their best to find Virginia and then solve her murder once her body was found. After that first month of her being missing, they could be fairly sure there were no witnesses that could solve the crime. So they turned to science. It was not necessarily called forensic science, but the expertise was strikingly similar, be it criminology, chemistry, or identification expert. Their efforts were surprisingly modern and probably all they lacked was today's tools.

Figure 5: The too similar funeral of Paula Magagna. The caption reads: Classmates mourn victim of sex fiend. Clad in white communion dresses, schoolmates of slain Paula Magana, solemnly escort the casket bearing her remains to St. Aloysius Church, Brooklyn, N.Y., for last rites. Thousands line the path of the cortege from the Magana home. Detectives in disguise mingled with the crowds in an attempt to ferret out the sex manic responsible for the crime. Credit line (ACME) 8/3/37.

Figure 6 San Diego investigators (Los Angeles Evening Herald.)

Chapter 5: Forensic Science

To its credit, the city of San Diego fell back on science to reinvigorate the investigation. While there may have been some 3rd degree as some claimed, the authorities did not resort to false confessions and a wrongful conviction. The only lawsuit claiming false arrest failed. If the evidence they had did not coincide with a suspect's potential guilt, they released that person. This despite having suspects under their microscope that could fit into the profile they were looking for, therefore making a false conviction more likely.

On the day Virginia's body was found Harry Wahlstrom, 28-year-old chicken rancher, was arrested because he was a dealer in leaf mold fertilizer. He was also, as mentioned, on probation for "mistreatment" of children. The authorities put 2 and 2 together and considered him a prime suspect. The Los Angeles Evening Herald summarizes the evidence at that time:

"A tiny sprig of mouldy oak leaves, mixed with heavy soil, [was] in the bottom of the burlap sack in which the body of the Brooks girl was found.

"Detectives admitted they had found nothing to link Wahlstrom with the crime.

"Other Developments followed thick and fast, as follows:

"1. Police rushed to Wahlstrom's chicken ranch, on the northeastern outskirts of the city, to probe into piles of leaf mold which Wahlstrom said he gathered in a nearby canyon and where, police believe, the body of the Brooks girl might have been temporarily buried before it was taken to Camp Kearny mesa in an automobile and hurled out into a patch of tall grass.

"2. Deputy Sheriff Blake Mason, who has followed scores of clues since little Virginia vanished from her home a month ago, carrying a bunch of Valentine day flowers to her teacher and a handful of valentine day cards for her chums, declared he expected to solve the murder mystery within 48 hours. Mason said he believed the body of the girl was concealed within 10 blocks of her home until it was taken out to the mesa.

"3. Tire marks found in the soft earth near the spot where the body was located by a wandering goat herdsmen provided police and deputies with their most dependable clue so far to the identity of the murderer. They did not compare with the tires of Wahlstrom's own car, police stated, but they learned that Wahlstrom had the use of another car, which they planned to check up.

"4. Although suspecting Wahlstrom because of his past conviction on charges of improper conduct with three small girls, police began a roundup of all known degenerates in San Diego and expected to grill them all regarding the Brooks murder. Fourteen such men were to be questioned, according to Chief of Police A.R. Hill.

"5. Fingerprint experts began a detailed examination of four story books, found in a sack near the Brooks girl's body, and identified as those the girl had under her arm as she left home last Feb. 11 for the Euclid school, about a mile away. It was believed smudges on the leaves [of the books] might be fingerprints. Also chemists were to examine traces of soil found between the pages in an effort to determine where the soil came from.

"6. Efforts to trace ownership of a glove dropped near the gruesome find and ownership of the burlap sacks in which the body and the books were stuffed had proven futile, but police continued to follow these slim clues, which might, by chance reveal identity of the murderer.

"7. Reports that a short, blond hair, presumably that of a man, had been found clutched in the hand of the little girl, were being run down by police. The report came from an unofficial source."

Chief Hill put every available officer on the hunt for the killer and stated he "was not satisfied with the autopsy performed yesterday by Dr. F. E. Toomey and County Chemist Earnest B. Mundkowski."

Both men who performed the autopsy opined their "findings would be of little aid to the police because of the decomposed condition of the girl's body." A cause of death could not be determined, according to them.

This might explain why Chief Hill accepted the help of experts from Los Angeles. Even after finding Virginia's body there was still nothing substantial that could lead investigators to a guilty individual. Chief Hill announced his men had run down more than 500 tips, "all given in good faith, but productive of no results."

One theory of the murder attempted to explain the various sightings in Arizona, Texas and possibly as far as Oklahoma. In this theory the killer drove around with the body in the back seat of his car. An obvious counterpoint was the girl was supposedly seen alive. Perhaps Deputy Mason, if this was his theory, was attempting to justify his time spent and arrests he made, or not.

Still, the theory went, the killer traveled about and "with the traditional weakness of the criminal he returned to the scene of his crime. Then, in desperation, lest his movement attract attention, he motored out to the mesa and abandoned the body without caring to bury it."

Chief Hill was not so sure.

"I am convinced," Chief Hill said, "that the man went to the mesa with no intention of concealing the body."

This disposal in San Diego was similar to the dumping of the bodies of the Martin sisters in 1924 and the Everett sisters and their friend in 1937 in that all 5 of those little girls could not be connected to a place that could be connected to a suspect. The authorities did all in their power to attempt to make a connection.

The LA Times offered some details:

"Another theory with greater support was that the killer never left the city and had been keeping the body, possibly in a shallow grave, and he was forced to move it due to increasing putrefaction."

The authorities must have considered the possibility that the killer feared his property being searched as well, and that would more or less rule out those under "strict surveillance" -- the usual suspects—because they would have been seen moving the body.

"Chief of Police Hill was hopeful that certain findings of County Horticulturist McLean regarding leaves found in the murder sack may prove of value. After reporting some of the leaves appeared to have been attacked by a plant disease peculiar to palms in a section of the county, McLean left on a secret mission. He was believed to be attempting to fix the exact location where the decayed leaves came from."

"The shallow grave theory had some support according to Chief Hill because the scales of dead leaves or leaf mold were found clinging to parts of the corpse. The plan now was to mount a house to house search concentrated in certain localities that had been under suspicion since the kidnaping. The skull presented a mystery however in that it was far more decomposed than the body. It had no flesh or hair when the condition of the torso, arms and legs were more intact yet still naturally decomposing. Some surgeons believed the skull was stripped by the forces of nature and they expressed the belief that the rest of the body might have been exposed for some time to the sun. Other surgeons, however, thought that the child was beheaded and that her murderer immersed the head in a solution of acid or quick lime in a cunning effort to remove all facial characteristics to prevent identification."

Leaving the books there for identification obviously defeated that purpose.

"The atrocious crime takes its place with the fiendish slaying of Marion Parker by William Edward Hickman as another of the most revolting in California's history," Chief Hill said, "and we intend to leave no stone unturned in our hunt for Virginia's murderer. He is somewhere in San Diego, we think, and we will find him. We must find him."

Figure 7: From the Los Angeles Evening Herald.

The parents were understandably prostrated by the morbid find. Both had been clinging to hope their daughter would be found alive. Rev. H.K. Holtzinger, who assisted in the funeral, tried to console them.

Police decided to start over by re-questioning the central witnesses. Among them were Mr. and Mrs. Brooks; George Moses, the goat herder who discovered the body, and Mrs. B. H. Ward, who lived about two miles from the Brooks home. It was Mrs. Ward who reported she saw an old Ford coupe parked over the curbing on University Avenue just west of Radio Road, while Virginia was approaching it on her way to school. The left front wheel of the auto had jumped the curbing and a young man in a gray suit and cap was sitting on the running board, reading a map. A large billboard was nearby. The man, police said, never reported seeing the girl pass him although she would have had to come within three feet of him on her way to the schoolhouse. The investigators declined to state whether they had asked Mrs. Ward to attempt to identify the suspect brought in earlier from Tacma by Deputy Mason.

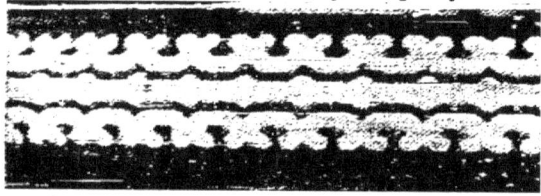

Figure 8 The tire tread as printed in the newspapers.

Following a different lead, the police impounded a light motor truck and on the floor inside were found several strands of human hair believed to be those of the Brooks girl, and its driver was held incommunicado pending analysis of the suspicious wisps.

The LA Times story of March 16 summed up this possible lead:

"The suspect and his truck were apprehended largely as the result of positive deductions that the child's body was transported to the mesa in that type of vehicle. Tire imprints left at the scene told investigators the front wheels of the death car were smaller than those in the rear, and only light trucks are thus equipped. All concerned in the manhunt are awaiting the findings of microscopic examinations of the hairs recovered from the truck. Police Chemist Rex Welch of Los Angeles is subjecting them to comparison with Virginia's own locks, and upon his report may depend a swift and unexpected solution of the baffling crime. Circumstances leading up to the apprehension of the truck driver were not revealed. Welch today completed his analysis of one of four hairs found in the half-clutched right hand of the slain girl. Three of them, he reported, were of Virginia's own dark brown tresses. The fourth is from the head of another person. Although it is impossible to determine whether the foreign strand is that of a man or a woman, Welch stated, it has been established as that of an adult. The telltale wisp of hair is that of a darker shade than those of the little victim.

"With the completion of his scrutiny of the hair found in the suspect's truck--providing it does not link the suspect with the crime--Welch will undertake similar comparison with the 'foreign' hair found in the child's hand, of ten other hair clews now in possession of police. Six of these are from the heads of suspects under surveillance here. The others were taken from suspects questioned at Los Angeles, El Centro and Salinas."

Welsh also had to analyze the books. Mr. Welch was likely saddened by the evidence found on the illustrations and handled them with care. Welch and Deputy Sheriff Gompert analyzed the books to classify soil found on some of the pages. They also did a chemical fuming process to reveal hidden prints but did not find any.[2]

---

[2] "Cyclopian fingerprints, enlarged after being photographed from the surfaces of glass, wood, steel, silver and even paper, are printed on the photo printer. If the prints have been made on paper he applies a little silver dust and the dust collects on the ridges of the print. The prints may be "set" by spraying with one chemical. The fumes from another chemical bring the fingerprint

On March 14, the LA Times reported on the tire track found by a man in a vacant yard.

"SUSPICIOUS TREADS DISCOVERED ON TIRES Two automobile tires, each having treads identical with that impressed on the ground near the location of the finding of the mutilated body of Virginia Brooks at San Diego, were turned over to police yesterday by Paul Dinus of 637 North Bronson Avenue. Dinus reported that he found the casings on a vacant lot near his home on the 2nd inst. [in or of the present month.] He placed them in his garage and gave them no more attention until newspaper photographs caused him to make a comparison. He then discovered that the tires had treads like that in the Brooks case. One of the tires is a 29 by 4.50 retreaded Goodrich Silvertown, and the other a 29 by 4.50 Goodyear Allweather. Both have been retreaded in the popular-type mold and bear the imprint of "Ed's Vulcanizing Works," which, police say, is not in Los Angeles. Despite the conflict in date the tires found by Dinus on the 2nd inst. and the body discovered on the 9th inst. "police have transmitted

---

out on paper like water soaking thru a blotter." Mason City Globe Gazette April 14, 1928.

the information to San Diego authorities. It is believed by investigators that the tires which left the impression on the mesa were there less than forty-eight hours before the body was found."

Virginia's body was found on the 10th of March, not the 9th, but the tires were found on the 2nd, so they could not have been on a vehicle later in March. Another false lead.

The San Diego tire investigation revealed the tires that left tire tracks in the mesa near the body were purchased from the Joe Shelly tire company. The exact date of sale could not be determined and the investigation went over receipts from the previous few months.

A naval officer purchased tires from a service station that were consistent with the tire tracks found at the crime scene. He was somehow familiar with the pattern, perhaps through some newspaper reports including pictures or by casts shown to him by the police. The service station attendant was able to give a good description to the police. Deputy Sheriff Gompert, identification expert, confirmed the tire matched the cast. This forensic lead led nowhere.

"I killed Virginia. I have performed a perfect crime. I am no degenerate. You will not find me: for I left no clew. This proves that I am superior. The Doctor."

That was the first note the police encountered from "The Doctor," and those who read John Douglas' books on criminal profiling will likely think that is exactly what the real killer would write.

There is a striking resemblance to *The Postcard Killer*, J. Frank Hickey (1910s) and Albert Fish (1920s) -- both atrocious killers of little children -- both men also wrote the victims' parents. But at first the police thought this note was just one of the many crank notes typical in a high-profile crime, as if people want a piece of the fifteen minutes of fame. A second note raised the stakes and the police had to pay close attention. Detective Lieutenant Sears thought the letter real and probably written by the slayer.

As the LA Times had it:

"The decision to concentrate the search on the author of the note came as somewhat of a surprise move for all concerned in the manhunt as all had first agreed the missive was but one of an inevitable flood of such communications from cranks."

The rumor was that the second note included a threat to kidnap another girl to demonstrate his superiority as a criminal. The first note was stuffed under a service station door near Virginia's home.

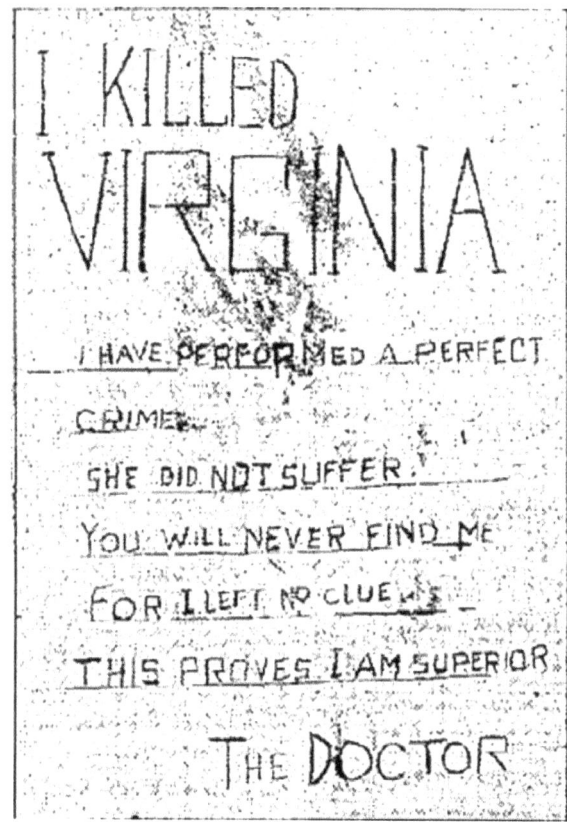

Figure 9. If this is a copy of the actual note, the wording is different than that quoted in the LA Times, March 19.

The second note did indeed threaten:
"I have defied your experts. Ha Ha! Another school girl will disappear within a week. Let mothers beware! The Gorilla."

The threat was half longhand, half printed in large letters on thick brown paper, the same as the doctor note and the second was mailed the same day the first note was left under a service station door. There was a service station at the corner of University and Radio road, so it could have been there.

Another note was left under the front door of the Brooks home in late March:

Of all the new developments, George Sears, lieutenant of detectives said he chiefly is interested in "The Doctor" note. This note was left beneath the front door of the Brooks home and was discovered there by Mrs. Brooks, who promptly turned it over to police. The contents were not divulged but the officer stated it made false allegations against some members of the family. It contained a dual threat to members of the Brooks family and police investigating the child's murder. "In almost every detail, particularly handwriting and the fact that it was written upon heavy brown wrapping paper, the latest note corresponded to the note signed 'The Doctor' and left under the door of a gasoline station near where Virginia was last seen alive," Sears said. The initial note was a boastful "confession" that the author of the letter not only had slain the child, but defied Police to capture him since he maintained he had committed the "perfect crime" and that the slayer never would be caught. "I believe both letters were written by the same person," Sears said.

Richard Daniels, 18, high school student who lived at 205 Laurel Street, was arrested for another most recent note left on a car in La Jolla. Two other students were suspected of being involved. He placed a note on an auto near the La Jolla Cove: "I killed Virginia Brooks. You will be next, so be careful. I shall not forget. The Doctor." Sears said, "This note and many others received by police have been written by cranks and practical jokers. Nevertheless, we must investigate each carefully and determine its exact significant to the case. Besides the terror spread to housewives of the city, the notes greatly hamper the work of police in seeking the actual killer."

Richard Daniels was free to participate in a horse riding club late in 1931, so perhaps the police never did figure out what they could charge him with. Daniels' note was written on white paper, however, not thick brown wrapping paper.

One startling headline highlights the additional pain and suffering the Brooks had to endure, the headline read:

"Rumor of Brooks' Arrest in Murder of Daughter False"

" Det. Lieutenant George Sears said the rumors

were malicious and false. The rumor was supposedly heard over the radio but no one would confirm which station. Brooks has been working steadily on construction work recently and has not been molested by police investigating the brutal slaying of his daughter. Brooks has given the police every assistance in seeking the murderer, according to Sears."

One of the strangest leads was one found in the Valencia Park section of National City, where a trunk thought missing from the "murder shack" in the hills above Virginia's home was found. Either written in pencil on a baby carriage found with the trunk, or written on a piece of paper attached to the baby carriage, was a note saying "This is my carriage-- Virginia Brooks." The two items were found at the dike directly south of Euclid school a couple of miles down Euclid Avenue. As the LA Times reported it:

TRUNK AND CARRIAGE STUDIED AS CLEWS

An abandoned trunk and baby carriage was found in San Diego on March 24 near the National City dike. "The trunk is believed to be the one missing from the deserted shack on Radio Road investigated as a possible "murder house." The baby carriage had on it a slip of paper upon which was written in pencil "this is the property of Virginia Brooks." They were turned over to Sears. There was a theory the child may have been crammed into the trunk by the murderer.

The carriage was taken to Brooks home for possible identification but it did not become a major clue, at least not a published solid lead.

The Hamilton Evening Journal published a full page magazine story entitled "And the Great Fear Followed 4 Laughing Girls Into Oblivion," with large pictures of the murder victims who suffered "the epidemic of murders," when "like slow poison, a great fear spread through the veins" of San Diego.

As pointed out earlier, there were other tragic murders the Southern California authorities had to contend with and the spree, or potential "murder cycle," began with the murder of Virginia Brooks. In mid-April Thomas Martinez took his wife and two children to Black Mountain north of the Kearney Mesa for a picnic. What was undoubtedly meant to be a happy family day turned gruesome when they found 17-year-old Louise Teuber, mostly nude and partially hanging from a tree. Her heels rested on the ground, leaving her body in a semi-sitting position with her buttocks about 2 feet in the air. Police investigated any potential connection to the Brooks case.

Dolly Bibbens, a gambler, was victim number three. She had been beaten to death in her home and a ring was torn from her finger. Number four was Hazel Bradshaw, who was found by children in

Balboa Park in central San Diego. She had been stabbed nine times. The article asks if the crimes were connected, and concludes it unlikely given the disparate evidence.

Another brutal murder the article does not mention occurred on the Todos Santos beach in Mexico the previous August. A Miss Marion Louis Kentle and a man named Francis Conlan were camping in a tent on the beach. She was stabbed 17 times and the police sought a gold-toothed man who had recently threatened others. Investigators followed up the theory that they and the "Brooks girl all were victims of the same slayer, a man with a degenerate demoniac passion to torture, kill and mutilate."

In response to these crimes, the state planned the expansion of its teletype service to San Diego, to be implemented by Senate bill No. 800. It would transverse from Yreka in northern California and down, through Imperial Valley, by way of El Centro, to San Diego, for a total of 18 centers that would communicate as fast as the newspaper wire service did.

On March 23rd the San Diego Union reported that Dr. J.F. White, local physician and surgeon, Schuyler C. Kelly, former county coroner, were conducting their own private investigation into the Brooks case when one of them found mud on his shoe when he returned to his office. Out of curiosity, he analyzed it under a microscope and found it identical to the mud on Virginia's shoes. Looking for where it came from, they returned to the hills they were searching and found a possible imprint of a body on the ground with the smell of death they hadn't noticed when searching the hills.

"Secluded in a canyon wedge and secluded from the eyes of passers-by, the lonely spot where lay the body of Virginia Brooks from the time she met death, which apparently was Feb. 11, until it was moved to Camp Kearny mesa was believed found yesterday. The location is about three-quarters of a mile from the Brooks home... and an equal distance from Euclid avenue school, to which Virginia was en route when she dropped from sight."

Police would not confirm it was the actual location until police chemist Welch completed his analysis of the soil and other debris found at the place.

Dr. Kelly reported these facts:
There was a perfect outline of where a body lain under a towering eucalyptus tree.
The presence of scrub oak bushes [and by most reports it was oak leaves in the sacks].
Foot prints.
A nearby water hole the girl's body could have

been submerged in.

An examination by a magnifying glass revealed imprints in the ground like the thread patterns in Virginia's coat.

Those who visited the area pointed out they experienced the same odor of death [as where the actual body was found].

In mid-March, San Diego got more help in the form of reinforcements. The Los Angeles county Sheriff's office sent down Undersheriff Frank Dewar and Capt. William Bright to join forces with local authorities and other out-of-town experts in hunting down the murderer of little Virginia Brooks. Capt. Bright was head of the homicide detail in Los Angeles.

At the same time, police searched for a mystery automobile.

"Meantime, police launched a hunt for a mystery automobile which they announced had been identified by nine persons as one which was seen to pause a short time on the Camp Kearney Mesa... then turn about and depart in the darkness. They declined to describe the car in detail but admitted it was a light open machine. It is understood they have been informed of certain distinguishing marks which may shortly result in its recovery."

"The manhunt swung again to the vicinity of the

spot where the girl's body was found, deputy sheriffs leading the visiting authorities on an expedition to deserted barracks at what once was the army cantonment. Every nook and cranny of these old frame structures is being searched for some telltale bit of evidence that may aid in pointing to the identity of the slayer."

Authorities also requested that all physicians in the county be on the lookout for the murderer based on "Welch's theory that the murderer may have contracted septicemia, a virulent blood infection, from handling the disintegrating corpse. Had he had a scratch on his hand at the time he moved the body to the mesa, it is pointed out, he probably could not have escaped the infection. Accordingly, physicians and hospitals have been requested to report suspicious cases of this nature."

The Coroner's autopsy released their official findings, announcing "it is our opinion that, due to absence of all the vital organs and the extensive loss of skin, muscles and other tissues, the cause of death cannot be determined." They point out also that there is "no evidence of injury to any of the bones, which are all present."

Photographs of more than 200 degenerate suspects taken into custody in Los Angeles in the last three years were sent to the authorities in the south, accompanied by detailed descriptions and a full account of their activities. The data were compiled by

Police Statistician Rhoda Cross and a staff of clerks at the request of Chief of Detectives Taylor.

There were remnants of 4-year-old newspapers in the gunnysack that referenced the real estate tract development around Virginia's home. That would coincide with the dates that the area's roads were extended and paved and Radio Road became 54th Street. This led investigators to concentrate on the area within a mile or two of her home. So there was a search of all abandoned shacks, homes, barns and whatever else they saw that might be a "killing laboratory."

"The belief that little Virginia's body had been hidden in a mould stack was based upon the fact the lower portion of her limbs were almost mummified, while the upper portion of her body had wasted. This led police to believe that the lower legs had become tanned by protruding from the sack and left exposed to sun and air.

"She may have been hidden in an attic or vacant storehouse, or buried in a shallow grave.

They were seeking "the "murder laboratory" where the killer disfigured her body, presumably with a searing acid or by boiling it in water."

"The disfiguration theory was strengthened by the discovery of a disjointed lower jaw bone to which bits of flesh adhered. However, an autopsy failed to find any trace of acid. The condition of the body was said to have made it impossible to determine what happened to the skin and hair.

"Police at first reported finding evidence of a basal fracture, indicating that the girl had been killed by a blow on the head." But that was refuted by a closer examination.

The Los Angeles Evening Herald recounts the conclusions of Los Angeles Police chemist Welch, who found the following:

1. Virginia Brooks was not decapitated or dismembered.

2. She was strangled to death ... garroted with a tourniquet made of stick and the flowing tie-straps of her dress. Police found the tell-tale stick in the burlap sack with the body and turned it over to Welch. Welch, with a microscope, then, found that the straps had been stretched and twisted, and so put the two discoveries together.

3. Welch also declared he found indisputable evidence that the little girl had fought her attacker to the end.

4. The body was not buried, but was concealed beneath moldy leaves and debris under shelter, either in a shed, barn, cellar or house, until it was taken and hurled into a clump of grass and brush on Camp Kearny mesa.

5. Wisps of hair clutched in the little girl's right hand probably are from the head of the man who killed her, and the murder probably took place on the day she was kidnaped near her home on Feb 11.

OTHER DEDUCTIONS

Following the paths of scientific observation, Chemist Welch reached many other deductions which he said proved the principal points he made.

Welch planned to use a valuable instrument of science in attempting to find telltale fingerprints or other evidence of the identity of the murderer on the story books which the child carried when she was abducted.

The books were to be placed in an air-tight container and subjected to chemical fumes which Welch, declared would bring out and make visible every spot and mark, even invisible ink marks. He also planned to subject the hairs found clutched in the little girl's hand to microscopic examination and declared he could determine even the gender of the person whose hair it was.

RECONSTRUCT CRIME

From his scientific observations, Welch reconstructed the crime in this order:

"Virginia was kidnapped or abducted on her way to school. The fiend probably took her to a house or

shack where he attempted to attack her.

"She fought back, desperately, scratching and clawing--and probably snatched out some of the man's hair.

"In a frenzy, the killer apparently grabbed this stick--a piece of stout wood, about eight inches long--and twisted the shoulder straps of her little gingham dress into a tourniquet which choked out her life.

"Virginia was either unconscious or dead when she was attacked--she fought to the end.

"Then the man carried her body somewhere and partly covered it with leaf mold and debris.

"The body was sheltered because its condition and the condition of the clothing, especially the shoes, indicate it was not exposed to recent heavy rains."

PARTIALLY CONCEALED

Long years of experience in the science of criminology, enabled Chemist Welch to deduce that the body was still warm when it was partially concealed, but not buried, in a pile of debris.

"This hastened the disintegration of the upper portion of the body," said Welch. The head was covered deeper than the torso, and the lower limbs were left exposed to the air.

"Agencies of decomposition immediately became active. The body must have been concealed the day Virginia vanished, for it would have taken at least 29

days for decomposition to have advanced so far.

"The killer, becoming frightened, apparently lifted the body out of its hiding place. In stuffing it into a gunny sack, the killer stripped most of the hair from the scalp and the arms became disjointed.

"Driving out to Camp Kearney mesa, the murderer hurled the gruesome bundle out onto ground, hoping that coyotes and other wild animals would complete destruction of the body.

ONLY SHORT TIME

"No animal had touched the remains, however, and this made it even more evident that the body had lain on the mesa only a short time before it was found by George Moses, the goat herdsman, and his dog.

Welch declared the type of beetle and the countless larvae that contributed to the disintegration of the body were of the type that multiplies and lives only in sheltered darkness. He said the little girl's garments, still shrouding her tiny body, provided 'natural facilities for incubation" of the strange vermin.

"But," Welch observed, "we have not yet caught the culprit, and that is the next step."

Given this summary of all their efforts it is obvious the authorities did all they could to solve this horrible crime. But they cannot be blamed for not knowing the new all-encompassing forensic science of today, and had they known, they may have caught their man. It was a factor 6 years later in the wrongful conviction and execution of Albert Dyer, but it was evidently not common knowledge in 1931. The conclusion explains this.

Figure 20: The Brooks, missing their daughter and sister. (Los Angeles Evening Herald)

Chapter 5: Conclusion?

On Thursday morning, March 12, 1931, the Los Angeles Times published the following editorial:

"THIS FIEND MUST BE CAUGHT

"Discovery of the mutilated body of Virginia Brooks, 10 years of age, near San Diego brings to light a crime that calls for the united effort of all Southern California for its solution. That the police, not only of San Diego but of every other community in Southern California, will do their best to identify and capture the slayer, goes without saying; but the clews are so few and so slight that their unaided efforts may easily go for nothing.

"The capture of the perpetrator of this crime is as important to the community as was the capture of Hickman—especially as it is a crime of a nature likely to be repeated. That he is probably a man of warped intellect does not necessarily mean that he is insane in a legal sense, or that his identity will thereby be more readily disclosed. It does mean that the necessity of his capture is made graver.

"A sadist or lust murderer at large is a continuing danger to every woman and child until he is put beyond possibility of doing further harm.

"The search should by no means be confined to San Diego. It is quite possible that the man is elsewhere—in fact, if he is as cunning as sadists usually are, he will not be discovered near the scene of the crime. Some small circumstance observed by a neighbor, a tradesman, a garage mechanic—a blood spot, a tire pattern, suspicious actions—may lead to the unraveling of the mystery and the capture of a man far more dangerous than a rattlesnake. The snake strikes only in self-defense, while the sadist seeks out victims with fiendish ingenuity.

"The police, without active co-operation, will find it an impossible task to do all the investigating that is likely to be necessary before this man is caught. It is up to everyone who notes any suspicious circumstance to turn the information in where it can be properly checked up. A discovery as accidental as that of Virginia Brooks' body, which was found by the merest chance, is likely to lead to the identification of the fiend. Multiply the few eyes of the police by the millions of the public and the chance to apprehend this fiend is multiplied proportionately. In a case of this kind everyone is a policeman.

"That the child was killed days ago, perhaps soon after her disappearance early in February, but that her body was not placed where it was found until a few hours before discovery, is the theory of the authorities. If so, the body must have been stored somewhere, and the finding of that somewhere will help to point toward the murderer. It apparently was taken there in some sort of a car; the discovery of that car is important.

"It was dismembered with some sort-of a knife, an ax, or other instrument; the finding of that instrument may give valuable information. These are the indications that are to be looked for.

"There never has been a perfect crime. It is impossible for a criminal not to make a mistake, to leave some trace of his identity. The clever Hickman left plenty of such traces. This San Diego crime is differentiated from the Hickman case by several particulars which it is important to keep in mind. Hickman kidnaped his victim for revenge and for ransom, and slew her through the cowardly fear of discovery. In all probability Virginia Brooks was kidnaped for the purpose of murder, with no thought of ransom in mind—though revenge as a possible motive need not be excluded.

"It is likely that she was picked for the victim by mere chance, and that the choice might easily have fallen upon any other child.

While these differences make the finding of the slayer more difficult they do not make it impossible. There have been mistakes made in this crime as in every other, and if they can be found they will lead unerringly to the culprit. When he is found he should be dealt with as the law directs."

The famed F.B.I. profiler John Douglas once stated he started his research with old newspaper articles. This could be a perfect example that led to his insights.

It is not fair to claim a conclusion pertaining to guilt is possible and it may never be possible to come to any conclusion at all, let alone a conclusion beyond a reasonable doubt. Some conclusions are possible, however. One most obvious one is that the good old days are largely wishful thinking. There were always dangerous predators parents and children should fear. Another conclusion is that forensic science was more sophisticated in 1931 than one might think.

One fact yet to be discovered was the distinct possibility that a serial killer may try to insert himself into the investigation. This was thought to happen in the murder of 4-year-old Joan Kubela in 1937, when the man who found her body was arrested and convicted for her murder; and for the conviction of Albert Dyer, as reported in *Colder Case*, when it was alleged he returned to the scene of the crime and tried to direct the investigation, and that was used against him.

In the Virginia Brooks case there were two potential suspects who admitted to being on the desolate murder road, twice. Both times they claimed they saw Virginia with a man driving a car, the second time when they were stuck in the mud. They also claimed it looked like she was held against her will. Then, with the "long arm of coincidence" they claimed they saw this same man along those desolate roads three weeks later after Virginia's body was found and they gave the "mean looking" man a ride into San Diego. The police investigated and found no merit to the accusation, but there were no reports of the police investigating these two men. Nor were there any reports that I could find that suggests any broadcasted description of Virginia Brooks having a broken tooth. The first report of it, before her body was found, was when these men claimed to notice it. After her body was found, at the inquest, this broken tooth is all there was to lead her mother to be certain it was indeed her child that was dead. She was that close to the child and was that aware of that detail.

Of all the sightings, only these two men got close enough to recognize that tooth. Did they see it on a frightened child as she peered at them out of a car window in terror? Or did they see it as they looked down at a frightened child and she looked back in terror? Did they direct attention away from themselves and try to get someone else convicted? Did they use their real names when reporting what they saw? Is it the long arm of coincidence that the same inland route leads past Camp Kearny mesa, where Virginia's body was found, past Black Mountain, where Louis Teuber's body was found, past Pomona where the photograph of John Brooks was found, and from there to the Ridge Route and Lebec where there was a gold mine sure to lead to the killer? Were they all the same men?

After all this time, there may not be anything conclusive enough to accuse anyone of this terrible crime of terrorism. But maybe the San Diego police cold case squad will take another look. Indeed, the case was never closed and the cold case got hot again on more than one occasion. That is the subject of the next chapter.

Chapter 6: Reopenings

The San Diego Union on Sunday Afternoon, May 3, 1931, posted this headline:

QUESTION SUSPECT AS GIRL IS FOUND MURDERED IN PARK
BODY OF MISS HAZEL BRADSHAW DISCOVERED IN INDIAN VILLAGE, SECRETED IN CLUMP OF WEEDS; VICTIM OF CITY'S FOURTH MURDER IN THREE MONTHS; STABBED 17 TIMES

The story covered the entire first page above the fold. So anyone who saw the paper would see nothing but this. There were two tiny little blurbs in the bottom right hand corner, if one squinted enough to read them, but for all intents and purposes, the front page was this story.

Needless to say, the authorities wanted to solve the cases and were doing all they could to do so. But cold cases become cold cases because the leads become dead ends. It didn't help that in mid-March, as the crime experts arrived to help the local authorities, the papers reported "the finding of what appeared to be a human lung in the swimming pool at Grape Day park, Escondido."

There was at last a big break at an El Cajon ranch almost 20 miles east of Virginia's home in 1935. Vernon Cooley, 56, a "white-haired El Cajon valley rancher," was under surveillance for about two months after "a complaint that he attempted to molest a 7-year-old girl while she and her parents and a younger sister were camped near his ranch.

"His hair matched the hair found in Virginia's hand when her body was found. But this is the first time it was said the hair was white. Frank Gompert, laboratory expert and criminologist of the LAPD classified it as the same type found beneath Virginia's fingernail. Also incriminating, investigators found the "exact type of leaf mould and palm leaves that were found clinging to the child's clothing when her body was found, and in the two gunny sacks in which the decapitated body had been stuffed. The palm leaves found on the body and sacks had a peculiar fungus growth, according to Gompert. The same peculiar fungus growth was found on palm leaves at the Cooley ranch Gompert added. Also at the Cooley ranch, investigators said, they found two light cars, one of which once perhaps was a sedan or touring car, and which might have been converted into a utility truck. At the time the girl's body was found, officers said they believe it had been hauled to the mesa in a light-weight machine, such as a Ford or a Chevrolet. The cars found at Cooley's ranch are 1928 or 1929 models, it was said."

Upon contacting Mrs. Cooley, separated for 10 years but never divorced from Vernon Cooley, she reported she left her husband because he had "peculiar" tendencies. She said, "After the Brooks girl's body was found on Camp Kearney mesa, my husband cautioned me never to let anyone question me about that particular case. He also cautioned me several times not to let anyone question me about anything in connection with him." At least that is her quote according to ADA Whelan.

She also told of a 3-year-old girl who appeared on the ranch under mysterious circumstances and then mysteriously disappeared. Cooley said she was a niece from Wisconsin and eventually he sent her back to her parents.

After initial questioning by some of Whelan's investigators, Cooley was alleged to have said during the ride back that "This is about the place where I last saw that little Brooks girl alive." That occurred near Country Club dr. and Jamul road, near Las Mesa. That would be about 15 miles east of the Brooks home.

One interesting detail pointed out was that the gunnysacks found with Virginia were "relatively new" and because of the "fresh" condition of the grass under them, the gunnysacks could not have been on top of the grass for long. The grass evidently even stood up again after picking them up as evidence. The gunnysack that Virginia was found in was even sewed shut as they usually are when filled. That might suggest the killer needed to make the sack look normal for those around him who would see it; or he feared someone coming upon it and peeking inside.

But then, how did the 4-year-old real-estate bits of paper get in the sack if they were "relatively new." Maybe he shoveled some of it from a pile into the sack as a camouflage so it would appear to be a normal sack. It might even camouflage the odor. That would suggest he was in the vicinity of enough people to be detected at least when moving the body.

The San Diego Union story of July 26, 1935, also points out there was "glazed piece of paper" found with her body that had a fingerprint on it. Was this clue held back by the police? Was it their ace in the hole? Did it slip out after so many years? The article also reveals that Welch arrived at his strangulation conclusion because of the "drawn" position of the body. That was proof of strangulation. It is still not clear why he thought she was "attacked after death, not before."

The article still claims little Virginia was "decapitated" despite Welch finding it was due to decomposition, not because of mutilation.

On July 27, 1935, The San Diego Union reports that Cooley was released:

"Vernon Cooley, 56, El Cajon valley farmer who was questioned most of Thursday night concerning the slaying of Virginia Brooks, 10, in 1931, was released on his own recognizance yesterday by Justice Dean Sherry.

"Release was made at arraignment on a charge that on May 21 he acted improperly with a 7-year-old girl. Preliminary hearing on the charge was set for Aug 8."

The article does not state how Cooley was able to absolve himself but his statements were checked and verified, so he must have had an airtight alibi. The charges against him pertaining to the 7-year-old girl were eventually dismissed as well. It would be interesting to know the back-story there.

There was another hot lead that seemed it was going to break the case in 1936. With every serious crime against a child, the San Diego authorities looked for a connection to their unsolved cases. The newspapers were always quick to make a connection. For example, on July 17, 1935, the San Francisco Chronicle printed the story of the arrest of Edward Earl Lambeth, former U.S. Marine, who "confessed under a lie detector last week to having attacked a 12-year-old. In conclusion the article ends with a summary of similar crimes:

"The Brooks girl was slain on the mesa outside of San Diego in 1931 and Louise Teuber, 17, killed later. In August, 1934, Celia Cota, 16, was criminally attacked and strangled."

The police wanted another chance to crack any of these cases and would get that chance with a request by Fresno authorities around New Year's Eve of 1935.

Fresno authorities thought the murder of 14-year-old Mary Louise Stammer in Fresno, CA, could be connected. Her mutilated body was found in her home several weeks earlier in December of 1935. George Brereton, under-sheriff of Fresno, asserted their suspect was also questioned in San Diego in 1931 during the Brooks investigation, so there was already some connection, and that is what they asked the San Diego authorities to look into. An article of Jan. 1, 1936 reported the Fresno undersheriff requested the San Diego authorities to investigate ships at the docks and locate the suspect. It was thought the San Diego authorities would have his prints on file if he was previously questioned regarding the Brooks case, but no record of his prints was found.

Fresno found their man anyway and he was about to be lynched. Three "cold-blood killers" were lynched in California in the previous two or so years.

The current suspect, Elton Stone, 30, on parole for theft, was said to have confessed to shooting

Mary Stammer through her window as she sat inside her home and read. There is accusation of him "disrobing" her has well. It is not clear how there could be some reports that she was mutilated without it being mentioned in the San Diego Union of Jan. 24, 1936. The record is slight. There was thumbprint found on broken glass outside of Mary's home, and the police were fingerprinting everyone in the neighborhood in an attempt to catch who the print belonged to. At first it was thought the killer was young, so the prints were taken of the younger males in the area, including high school students, then the investigation expanded to older males. Everyone in the area volunteered their prints except for 13 men. One of the 13 was Elton Stone and he was pointed out by a senior citizen that lived in the neighborhood of the killing.

Mary Stammer was the daughter of Walter H. Stammer, a prominent Fresno attorney and Stone claimed he killed his daughter out of revenge. But Walter Stammer stated he had no record of dealings with Elton Stone and he did not know why there would be a grudge. Police thought Stone was just trying to justify the killing. Stone was taken from the county jail to Folsom Prison from Fresno for his own safety and newspapers reported him being cocky about it. There were serious threats of lynching.

He was taken before the Grand Jury of Fresno on Jan. 24, where the county grand jury returned an "indictment charging Elton M. Stone, 31, former convict, with first degree murder in connection with the death of Mary Louise Stammer."

He was then rushed back to Folsom Prison. Given his confession to "the most fiendish crime in Fresno history," it would be no surprise that the authorities planned to interrogate him on the murder of Mrs. Berth Blagg (1934), "in a somewhat similar crime," and the murders of Virginia Brooks and Louis Teuber.

It was no surprise that the "Lynching Threats For Girl's Slayer" also grew. The sheriff's office had to smuggle him into arraignment for fear a mob would get him. One noted threat was that the legal system had "about 48 hours" to do justice or it would be done as were done the lynchings in Yreka and San Jose.

Before dying Mrs. Blagg wrote the name of her murderer: Stone. But when asked to write the first name she wrote "Clayton." "Clayton Stone proved to be a 14-year-old schoolboy, honor student and Boy Scout." So the police believed the dying woman was confused. And Elton Stone lived near her place, and had a record for theft, and someone said they saw him near the Blagg home "shortly before the murder."

Under questioning, Stone claimed he was in custody because Mrs. Blagg wrote his name. "Nobody tipped the police to check my fingerprints. Nobody informed on me. The police just checked up on everybody that had been questioned in the Blagg case and they got me."

"Have you anything to tell us that you think we should know?" Investigator Ford asked.

"Not yet," Stone replied.

"What did other people you talked with think about the Stammer Crime?" he was asked.

"They said the guy that did it ought to be strung up," Stone answered casually.

"Did you agree with them?

"Sure, you bet."

"Do you still agree with them?

"Sure."

So amid the threat of lynching -- somewhat similar to the threat of lynching in the Albert Dyer case, when he so wanted to plead guilty (and get probation) -- Elton Stone was taken into court for arraignment and was allowed to plead guilty. Albert Dyer was not allowed to plead guilty in 1937 and that is why there is an official record in his case buried deep in the California State Archives. That record strongly argues for a wrongful conviction and a wrongful execution. The death sentence of S.C. Stone, no relation, in the 20s was commuted based on the record. The record here is that Elton Stone was executed on June 12, 1936.

Elton Stone is #89 of *Folsom's 93: The Lives and Crimes of Folsom Prison's Executed Men*, by April

Moore. In her pithy summary of the crimes she explains why the authorities were convinced Stone was a serial killer and was responsible for other murders:

"In July 1934, Mrs. Bertha Blagg was raped and bludgeoned while she slept. Partially paralyzed and unable to speak, Bertha wrote a name on a piece of paper: Clayton Stone. When the fourteen-year-old Boy Scout and schoolmate of her two sons was cleared of all wrongdoing, the case became a mystery. Blagg died a week after the attack. Nina Gates Johnson, who also lived in the area, narrowly survived an attack in her bedroom in 1931."

It turned out that Stone lived near all three women and his thumbprint matched the print on a piece of broken glass from the killer breaking into the house after shooting Mary from outside. He confessed. Sometimes, probably most times, confessions are legitimate. The California Supreme Court's ruling affirming his death sentence, a very short unanimous opinion, is in the appendix.

The San Diego authorities never gave up and thought they had their man again in 1946.

On February 3, 1946, The San Diego Union ran a story with this headline:

"POLICE SEEK FOR CONFESSION IN 15-YEAR-OLD BROOKS CASE."

The article covers the start of a series of events that would land an accuser in jail and set the accused free. San Diego Dist. Atty. Thomas Whelan was sure he had his man this time. A reliable source told him a man named Owen Jack Hayes, 65, a former bootlegger, confessed that he accidently ran down Virginia Brooks while she walked to school. He hid her death for weeks and then dumped her body. There was a search all along the coast for Hayes and he learned the police wanted to talk to him after receiving a letter from his wife, but he didn't know why. After driving from his home in Sacramento to his former home in San Diego, Hayes turned himself in to the police station saying they wanted to talk to him. He and the investigators all visited his old haunts at 4276 Altadena, "only a few blocks from the home once occupied by the Brooks family." While meeting with investigators, including Mr. Whelan, they chatted about old streets and new developments in the neighborhood before he was taken back to the police station and grilled for an entire weekend.

While at his former house, "particular emphasis was placed on the soil and vegetation in the backyard, as investigators attempted to link with [that] one [horticulture] clue in the sensation slaying."

Hayes was partially deaf, but he was able to point out where he had terraced the yard and pointed out the trees he had planted. He did not deny he was in San Diego in 1931 and that he owned a Ford pickup truck, but the said, "I don't know nothing but what the newspapers said. I don't know nothing about this. I thought they was kidding me." He thought it was about a traffic violation or something.

When told of his right to remain silent, Heyes chuckled and said, "I don't know what to say about that." But he was nervous at first and knew this was a serious accusation.

He admitted he was questioned in 1931 before Virginia's body was found, and when Whelan asked if he was under suspicion then, Hayes said, "Everybody was. I remember some Boy Scout looked in my basement."

He was then confronted with the reason for the present suspicion. A navy petty officer that Hayes supposedly knew at the time claimed Hayes admitted to him about 10 days after Virginia's body was found that he accidently struck the girl with his truck. He said Hayes told him about it when he, Stroud, visited his home to purchase some liquor.

"I never hit anybody with my car. The only thing I ever hit was a little black bear near Lake Tahoe," Hayes said.

The mentioned navy petty officer was Dennis Dent Stroud, 42, chief boatswain's mate stationed on the U.S.S. Oglethorpe.

Countless men were arrested for suspicion of murder, fingerprinted and grilled, and then released. Not Hayes. He was booked and arraigned by Judge A.F. Molin "on a charge of murder in connection with the slaying in 1931 of 10 year old Virginia Brooks." He was ordered held without bail for preliminary hearing February 27th.

Dist. Atty. Whelan claimed to have found evidence that would corroborate Petty Officer Denis Dent Stroud's accusation that Hayes confessed to the slaying of Virginia. Whelan pointed out that Hayes lived in San Diego at the time of the murder and lived one half mile from the Brooks home.

Whelan also had some witnesses now living in the Midwest who used to live in the Hayes neighborhood, but he refused to say who or what they might know. Since the Hayes house we near the corner of Trojan and Altadena, it is easy to wonder if one of these witnesses was Mrs. Martin, who said she saw Virginia walking with a man. She was the one that described them both so well.

By the time of his arraignment, Hayes took it all casually, smiling and outwardly confident, and he seemed unmoved by the seriousness of the charges. Hayes claimed Stroud wanted to get "revenge for some imagined wrong he thinks I done him." His alibi was that he was not home that day because he was out delivering whisky to "two prominent El Centro people whose names were not disclosed."

"I might get them to establish an alibi for me, but may be they won't want their names brought into anything like this," police quoted Hayes.

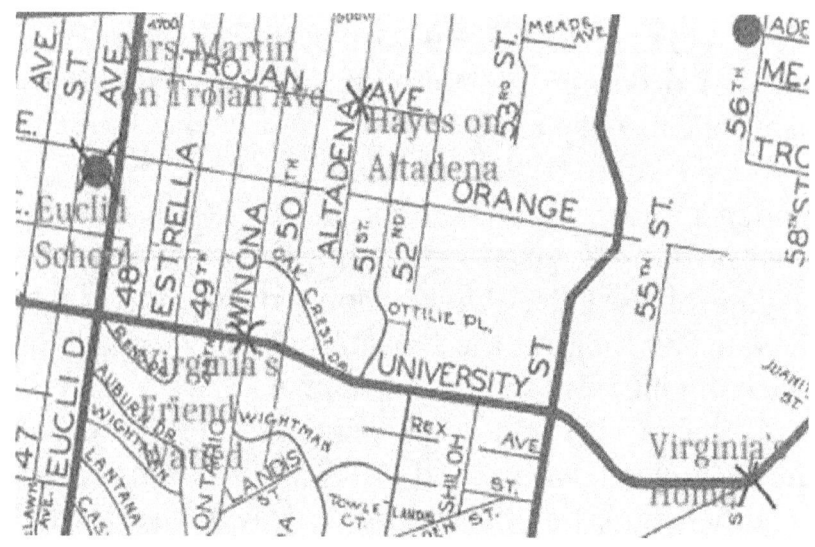

Figure 31 Hayes lived near Mrs. Martin, who lived on Trojan Ave. and said she saw Virginia walking with a man and she described them both well.

Dist. Atty. Whelan had a wrinkle in the case he couldn't iron out. Detective Lieutenant Ed Dieckmann was the head of the police homicide detail, and in a letter to Whelan he requested the charges be dismissed because he found "'new evidence' that tends to tear down the story told by Naval Chief Dennis Dent Stroud." So without giving the details Dieckmann asked that the charges be dismissed and Hayes be freed. It was reported that Stroud thought there was a "$50,000 reward for the conviction of the girl's slayer." Maybe that had something to do with it. District Attorney Whelan decided to hold Hayes through the preliminary hearing despite Detective Lieutenant Ed Dieckmann's request to have the charges dismissed.

So Whelan's response was that he "will go slow" regarding the detective's request. He was still trying to get Virginia's father to come from Portland, Ore. to testify for legal reasons. That was because the death certificate had expired by then and Whelan would have to prove she was dead. Virginia's mother had passed in 1935. Maybe she died of a broken heart.

In a twist to challenge a movie plot, a friend of Stroud came forward and stated he had heard the same story from Stroud about Hayes two years previously. J.W. Vance, navy engineer and shipmate of Stroud, told San Diego police he was "associated with the Huntington Beach police department before the war and now is on the department's eligible list." Vance said Stroud twice told the same story about Hayes, once in Palau and again nearly a year later, repeating it word for word.

The two bunkmates decided to implicate Hayes. The two men agreed that whichever of them got back to San Diego first would report the story to the police. When subpoenaed to appear for the preliminary hearing, however, Stroud refused to accept it. He did not have to accept a civil subpoena while on federal navel base land in San Francisco and so refused to do so, saying his commanding officer would not release him from navy duty. He said he would have had to go A.W.O.L. to accept it. Without Stroud's testimony, the case fell apart.

After 28 days in jail on the murder charges, Hayes was released on Feb. 27, the reason being Whelan thought Stroud was motivated by the reward. The problem was there wasn't any $50,000 reward for the conviction of Virginia's murderer. Stroud just thought there was. So what part did Vance play? Were they going to split the reward? Did Hayes really confess that but Stroud only thought it worth speaking out about it if there was a reward? Stroud was charged with obstructing justice and "giving false and misleading" information regarding the Hayes charges. He did not have the right to refuse to accept the charge and was taken into navy custody on the arrest warrant and then taken to San Diego. So on March 11, 1946, exactly 15 years after Virginia's body was found, Stroud was in custody in relation to the Virginia Brooks murder. "From what he told me, I still believe Jack Hayes is the guy," Stroud said.

On March 30, 1946, the charges against Stroud were dropped. He was turned over the navel authorities for discipline.

In June of 1947, there was this article headline: "Virginia Brooks Slaying Revived." The story was of an anonymous phone call to the Kansas FBI and a man reported he was sure "he had information which would identify the murderer of the San Diego girl." The FBI of course relayed this information to San Diego authorities. The call was traced and the man was to be questioned, but nothing came of it.

Was this the same Midwest witness relevant to the Hayes charge? Did someone in the Midwest expect a conviction but then none came, so it simmered all undone until he made the anonymous call?

The only thing certain is that the Virginia Brooks case is still a colder case and her killer remained free to strike again.

Apendix: *People v. Stone, 6 Cal.2d 62*

[Crim. No. 3986. In Bank. April 2, 1936.]

THE PEOPLE, Respondent, v. ELTON M. STONE, Appellant.

COUNSEL

Arthur C. Shepard, Edward L. Kellas and A. W. Carlson for Appellant.

U.S. Webb, Attorney-General, and Dan F. Conway, District Attorney, for Respondent.

OPINION

THOMPSON, J.

The defendant was indicted for murder. At the time of arraignment, it appeared that he had not secured counsel. The court explained to him the charge and the possible penalty therefor and, upon defendant's request, appointed counsel. After arraignment, ample opportunity was extended defendant for consultation with the two lawyers appointed by the court, before he was required to enter his plea. He pleaded guilty to the charge and the court took evidence for the purpose of ascertaining whether there were any facts which would justify the court in imposing a life sentence instead of the extreme penalty. The trial judge concluded that there were no such facts and sentenced defendant to be hanged.

The appeal is here because, in 1935, the legislature amended section 1239 of the Penal Code by inserting the following sentence:

"When judgment of death is rendered, upon any plea, an appeal is automatically taken without any action by the defendant or his attorney."

[1] At the time set for the oral argument on this appeal, both of the attorneys for defendant appeared and stated that in their opinion there was no ground upon which a reversal could be based and that in truth, the entire proceeding was fair and in conformity with the law. We deem it unnecessary, under the circumstances, to detail the evidence. Suffice it to say that we have read the testimony, including a full and apparently complete confession by the defendant. It demonstrates beyond question that defendant is guilty of a deliberate and premeditated killing of a high school girl in Fresno, under peculiarly aggravated circumstances. It follows that the judgment should be and it is hereby affirmed.

Waste, C.J., Langdon, J., Conrey, J., Curtis, J., Seawell, J., and Shenk, J., concurred.

Visit the Author's Amazon Series Page

The Colder Case Series